SEMEIA 34

Biblical Hermeneutics in Jewish Moral Discourse

Guest Editor of this Issue:
Peter J. Haas

© 1985

by the Society of Biblical Literature

SEMEIA 34

Copyright © 1985 by the Society of Biblical Literature

All rights reserved. No part of this work may be reproduced or transmitted in any form or by any means, electronic or mechanical, including photocopying and recording, or by means of any information storage or retrieval system, except as may be expressly permitted by the 1976 Copyright Act or in writing from the publisher. Requests for permission should be addressed in writing to the Rights and Permissions Office, Society of Biblical Literature, 825 Houston Mill Road, Atlanta, GA 30329, USA.

ISSN 0095-571X
ISBN 1-58983-223-X

Printed in the United States of America
on acid-free paper

CONTENTS

Contributors to This Issue.................................... v

Introduction.. 1

Moral Value and Literary Traditions:
The Case of the Succession Narrative
    Douglas Knight 7

Response to Douglas Knight:
But How Does it Happen? A Note on "Predecessors and Successors"
    Lou H. Silberman 25

To Speak, How to Speak, and When Not to Speak:
Answers from Early Rabbinic Stories
    Joel Gereboff 29

Response to Joel Gereboff:
When Speech is No Speech: The Problem of Early Rabbinic Rhetoric as Discourse
    Jack N. Lightstone 53

Toward a Semiotic Study of Jewish Moral Discourse:
The Case of Responsa
    Peter J. Haas 59

Response to Peter Haas:
Semiotics and Jewish Ethics
    Daniel Patte 85

Jewish Legal Interpretation:
Literary, Scriptural, Social and Ethical Perspectives
    David Ellenson 93

Response to David Ellenson:
A Living Tradition: Ongoing Jewish Exegesis
    Elliot N. Dorff 115

Response to David Ellenson:
Law, Ethics and Ritual in Jewish Decision Making
Daniel Landes 123

CONTRIBUTORS TO THIS ISSUE

Elliot N. Dorff
University of Judaism
15600 Mulholland Drive
Los Angeles, CA 90077

David Ellenson
Hebrew Union College-
Jewish Institute of Religion
3077 University Drive
Los Angeles, CA 90007

Joel Gereboff
Department of Religion
Arizona State University
Tempe, AZ 85287

Peter J. Haas
Department of Religious Studies
Vanderbilt University
Nashville, TN 37235

Douglas Knight
Vanderbilt Divinity School
Vanderbilt University
Nashville, TN 37235

Daniel Landes
Yeshiva University of Los Angeles
9760 W. Pico Blvd.
Los Angeles, CA 90035

Jack Lightstone
Department of Religion
Concordia University
Montreal, Quebec H3G 1M8
Canada

Daniel Patte
Department of Religious Studies
Vanderbilt University
Nashville, TN 37235

Lou H. Silberman
Department of Oriental Studies
The University of Arizona
Tucson, AZ 85721

INTRODUCTION

This volume is a study of rabbinic moral discourse. It proceeds from a single proposition, namely, that the moral system of any generation is fashioned out of the legacy it receives from the past. This statement has two ramifications which we shall explore in the following pages. The first is that each new generation is born into a community which already has a system of moral rules and which presents these rules to the new generation as part of its heritage. The second is that this new generation must receive that system and give it its own compelling articulation. Moral socialization then is a two-part process. The older generation articulates its moral code and presents it to the rising generation. This generation receives these standards, interprets them in light of its own realities, and accepts them as its own. This particular appropriation then becomes the legacy passed on to the next generation.

It follows from this model that understanding the moral universe of an ongoing tradition, such as Judaism, requires that we pay attention not only to how moral rules and standards are stated by the canonical authorities of each generation, but also how these are taken over and modified by succeeding generations. Our program here is to make a preliminary trace of the outlines of that process within Judaism from its beginnings in Scripture, through the earliest rabbinic literature and to classical rabbinic responsa of the medieval and early modern periods. In all cases our focus will be on the processes by which an older articulation of morality is received, adapted to new circumstances, and then transmitted to succeeding generations. Our goal is to begin to understand the rhetorical devices that characterize the Judaic attempt to express moral truths.

The essays collected here can be read in a number of different ways. They present first of all, as we said, a literary history of rabbinic moral discourse from Scripture to modern times. This is accomplished by examining representatives of the major literatures in which Scriptural and rabbinic ethics are articulated. They survey begins with Scripture, since this is foundational to all later systems of Jewish ethics, rabbinic or otherwise. It is in this document, itself a composite, that our problematic receives its first articulation. We next turn to Mishnah, the foundational document of rabbinic Judaism. The Mishnah, edited in its received form in the early third century, establishes the tradition of discourse that stands behind the Talmud, and so becomes characteristic of rabbinic Judaism. Along with Scripture, it provides the literary foundation for all later rabbinic moral speculation. Classical rabbinic Judaism emerges in the tenth century and develops as its particular mode of literary expression the legal rescript (responsum). These texts attempt to frame legal and moral rulings that carry forward the perceived principles of Scripture and Talmud, while articulating these in contemporary terms. Our last two articles examine this literature, using a medieval text (the third essay) and an early modern one (the fourth essay). In all cases, the reader is asked to consider not the moral issues at hand, but more particularly how each text proposes to communicate those issues. The theory here is that we learn as much about a culture's ethics from how it frames matters as from its actual concrete decisions. We have, then, a literary history of rabbinic moral discourse that begins in the roots of the tradition, Scripture on the one hand and Mishnah on the other, and traces the development of ethical rhetoric through the characteristic rabbinic moral texts, the responsa.

On a second level, the authors of our essays want to explore how such texts from various epochs of the rabbinic tradition are to be read and studied as moral texts. That is, each essay has as its task to focus on a particular text and to show how that kind of text can be studied in an academically responsible way. It is for this reason that each major essay is followed by at least one response. We wish not only to present these texts to the reader, but we wish to have the authors, and the reader, engage in thinking about the methodological issues raised by these diverse documents.

For this reason, each contributor was asked to concentrate on a single methodological problem raised by the text at hand. Douglas Knight raises the seminal issue of this volume in relation to the Scriptural corpus, namely, how can the process of the transmittal of morality be adduced from ancient written documents. His answer, which is a theorem for the rest of the volume, is that any generation's view of the world can be passed on only if it is done in a way that makes it self-evidently true to the receiving generation. We need to see the Scriptural material as a sort of snapshot, showing us how, at some point in time, one generation proposed to transmit its wisdom to the next. But, as Professor Knight points out, the process of the transmission of moral values requires a receiver, not just a transmitter. The passing generation may formulate matters well, but they still must be accepted and absorbed if they are to continue to live. So the transmittal of moral values in literature does not happen *in* a generation, but *between* generations. It is to this problem, and the methodological issues it raises, that Lou Silberman so eloquently directs our attention.

The dynamics of ethical transmittal stand also behind the analysis of Mishnah, and its companion Tosefta, by Joel Gereboff. Here we see the process at work in the other great literary pillar of rabbinic Judaism. As was the case in Scripture, we see the early rabbis struggling here to formulate their moral insights in a way that will compel the reading generations to accept these as their own. In this case, as in Scripture, moral virtues are not proffered as philosophical truths, but as exemplary deeds and sayings of the heroes of the rabbinic tradition. There is, Gereboff points out, a deeper literary, and so symbolic, structure at work here. It is in light of this assertion that we are to read Jack Lightstone's reponse. It has all too often been taken as granted that the deeds and sayings recorded in Mishnah (and the other rabbinic texts) really happened. That is, these texts are not literary structures, but objective reports of the truth. Professor Lightstone's response makes explicit what Professor Gereboff assumes, namely, that we are dealing with a mode of symbolic transmittal of values, not with what "really" happened. Our attention must be not on whether or not Aqiba really said X, but on what it means (or is supposed to mean, Professor Silberman's problem again) for us to say that Aqiba said X. Attention remains on literary strategy as a mode of moral teaching.

This brings us to the last two essays of the volume, both of which deal with the classical, and characteristic, rabbinic literature, the responsum. These texts assume the utter validity of Scripture and Mishnah-Talmud, and attempt to create legal and moral rules on the basis of these texts. To do so, of course, requires the creation of a new literary genre, one in which Scripture and Talmud on the one hand, and contemporary realities on the other, can be brought into conversation. Again what both essays point out is that the important issue for understanding moral discourse is not what the rulings are, but how they are expressed. As in Scripture and in Mishnah, the very format of the text communicates moral values, quite independently of the particular ruling at hand. The receiving generation is instructed in the meaning and nature of the moral life simply by being presented with moral rules in just this way.

These last two essays approach the methodological problems of studying this literature from two different angles. The first deals with the literary character of these documents. It proposes a way of reading these texts which will reveal the common assumptions about the nature of morality which the author (and presumably the reader) hold. There is, this essay asserts, a common universe of discourse established by the text, and so between the comprehending reader and the author, which gives a certain content to the notion of what ethics is. For the text to work, certain convictions about ethics must be held in common by the writer and the reader, or at least be transmitted by the writer to the reader. The response by Professor Patte points out how these symbolic and subterranean characteristics of the text can be understood in terms of structural literary analysis. In so doing, he sharpens the methodological grid through which the structure of these texts might be adduced and understood. The last essay returns us to the generative problem pointed out by Douglas Knight, namely, how a moral statement, in particular a responsum, is appropriated by the receiving generation(s). David Ellenson powerfully reminds us that the creation of any moral value always takes place within a concrete social setting. Moral principles and rules are not simply received from the past but are interpreted, adapted, and reused by successor generations. The way in which these forces impinge on the creation of a new moral text is examined in Professor Ellenson's study. His essay thus provides the woof to Professor Haas's warp. In Professor Haas's essay we see the structural elements that shape the character of other responsa literature in general. In Professor Ellenson's essay, we see how this form is given content and texture by a particular person at a particular time dealing with particular problems. In terms of this dynamic, the responses by Professors Dorff and Landes are helpful. They remind us that the process of adapting and adopting moral discourse from the past is a complex business. The warp that is the received tradition is hardly uniform or univocal, as Professor Dorff reminds us. The rabbinic decision to shape its own morality in terms of the tradition opens up a whole range of problems. Texts must be chosen, interpreted, and applied, none of which activities have self-evident solutions. There is always interaction between the text to be chosen and the context of the chooser. What this means is that the successor generation never receives a tradition empty-handed, but as the *successor* always has a system of convictions which must affect him even at his first reading of a text from the predecessors. This is a point brought out by Professor Landes in the last essay of the volume. In its own way it brings us back to the starting point, the difficult question of understanding *how* morality is passed on from generation to generation. These essays are an attempt to identify and articulate that problem, and also to search for avenues of solution.

This volume can be read in a third way as well. It is designed to serve as a textbook for the study of Jewish ethics. In this it departs radically from existing models for doing so. Our reasons for formatting matters as we have needs explanation. The emphasis on literary form explored here carries with it the conviction that any attempt even to explain Jewish ethics must take account of how Jewish moral discourse actually is structured. As we shall see in the last two essays, Jewish ethical discourse takes the form of a careful analysis of the logic of the dilemma in light of Scripture and other religious literature. It is a discourse which forces the reader him or her self to struggle to find the proper meaning of the classical texts. This volume is designed to duplicate that process. It begins in all cases with a specific text. This text is studied to determine what light it can throw on our general understanding of the problem. These studies are themselves subjected to critique and analysis. The effect, then, is to lead the reader through the mental process of Jewish learning while engaged in the study of Jewish ethics.

It is concerning this last point that this project hopes to break new ground. Studies of rabbinic ethics routinely take one of two forms. Most writing on Jewish ethics has been descriptive, "the" Jewish view of this or that. In some cases (I am thinking here especially of authors like J. David Bleich, Fred Rosner and David Feldman among others) these are written within the framework of classical Jewish ethical writings. That is, they describe the content of the tradition from within the tradition itself. While this gives us an accurate account of what has been said, it does not provide a framework for useful comparison with systems outside of rabbinic Judaism. On the other hand, there are accounts of what Jewish moral views are, or should be, written largely from the perspective of people outside the classical system. While these form good bases for comparison, since they are written in the semantic universe of modern American academia, they do not, for that same reason, accurately represent the nature of the tradition. So only a filtered rendering of Jewish ethics is available for comparison. The most blatant example of this are those attempts to find the "essence" or "core" of Jewish ethics and present these as disembodied philosophical postulates. This not only presents Jewish ethics in terms of an alien ethical system, but distorts the very character of what Jewish moral discourse is all about.

The project presented here is an experiment. It hopes to discover a way of presenting Jewish ethics that is both faithful to the style and content of the tradition and that allows for some meaningful comparison. Our theory is that the most satisfactory way of doing comparative ethics is to compare system to system, not this ruling to that ruling or this axiom to that axiom. Our assumption, then, is that the studies undertaken here have found a mode of discourse that accurately reflects the nature of the subject matter and yet partakes of a larger universe of discourse that allows for comparison. That is, we want to be able to study what is particularly *Jewish* about Jewish moral discourse, and yet also be able to use this to help us better understand the nature of moral discourse in general, and so better to appreciate the ongoing human attempt to shape a moral life of which the Jewish effort is a part.

MORAL VALUES AND LITERARY TRADITIONS: THE CASE OF THE SUCCESSION NARRATIVE (2 SAMUEL 9–20; 1 KINGS 1–2)

Douglas A. Knight
Vanderbilt University

ABSTRACT

A study of the ethics of the Hebrew Bible embraces not only the final written text but also the long process during which the traditions behind it originated and developed into their ultimate form. The process reveals a continual effort by all generations to respond to their own particular situations both through recourse to the past and through creative engagement with their present circumstances. Moral values are thus seen to emerge as moral problems are faced, and the literary traditions convey these values from one period to the next. Using the Succession Narrative as an example, this essay analyzes the different roles played first by the predecessor generation and then later by the successor generation in the use of tradition to affect moral conduct. Such a process of moral determination throughout the course of biblical history, it is suggested, can be seen as a precedent of the ways in which Jewish ethics in the postcanonical period draws creatively and critically on biblical norms and principles.

I. THE CONTEXT

There are two main alternatives, set at opposite ends of a continuum, for approaching the Hebrew Bible as a literature of ethics. On the one hand, it can be viewed as a *product* or entity that is fixed, final, and—for some—authoritative. Focus thereby falls on its present state, its facticity as written text rather than any prehistory of contextuality which it might have had. Moral values can accordingly be seen to inhere in it as objective realities, ascertainable through careful study of the text without reference to the multiple social realities which might have produced these value statements. As the primary authority and guide for the moral life of believers, the text has often been and still is probed for principles and specific directives, and any objectionable positions or inconsistencies on a given moral issue in the Bible can in the process be harmonized, overlooked, or denied. Thereby the Bible is made to function as a repository of ethical truths which need only to be identified or discovered and then applied. To be sure, it is possible for any given group of people to accumulate a set of interpretations about what these moral principles are and how they are to govern behavior, and such a set can in turn assume an importance alongside that of the Bible.

At the other end of the continuum is an approach which emphasizes the *process* which led up to the Bible as a fixed and final product. This view, in a strict sense, is a result of the rise of the historical-critical method since the Age of Enlightenment, although it is hardly the case that this approach has been dominating the scene among all persons who make use of the Bible in moral decision-making. By "process" we mean the historical development of the biblical literature in light of all the varying factors which affected it. Accordingly, the moral aspects of this literature are seen to be not fixed truths solidified in canonical form but rather the variable decisions and values of innumerable people throughout some thousand years of Israelite and early Jewish existence. While an objective value theory tends to underlie the perception of the Bible as product, a historically relative value theory—whether these values are considered to be subjective or relational—seems more often to be operative when one focuses on the Bible as process. As the social and economic situations changed for the ancient Israelites, their moral responses to specific problems could correspondingly change also.[1] The Bible which emerged at the end of the process has, by choice and circumstances, retained ample evidence of this variety, an intricate complex of moral postures and judgments which an ethical study of the biblical tradition must fully consider.

The two alternative approaches which have just been schematized are, it must be stressed, opposite ends on a continuum, and in reality it is more common to see some modified version of one or the other than to see either in its pure form. The above description, however, should serve to highlight several aspects of both approaches. The present essay, in its preference for the second approach, advocates that the ethics of the Hebrew Bible encompasses the whole range of the biblical period—to the extent that it can be reconstructed—from the earliest evidences of moral judgments and conduct on down to and including the final text of the canon. While Jews, Christians, and others since then have tended to consider only the canonical text as authoritative, it is equally possible to elevate in importance the values, attitudes, and practices evident in earlier traditions. To be sure, the final form of the text is itself a dynamic entity with power to stimulate creative response among those who turn to it, but this power is in no small measure due to the process in which many people in various generations contributed to the makeup of potentially any page of this text. In a word, the formation of tradition and the formation of values tended to go hand in hand, and the final text is in a real sense a monument to this process.

The details of this developmental process interest us at this point, and for a very clear reason. Just as we ourselves tend to look to past tradition—such as the Bible, among other things—for direction and legitimation as we reach our moral decisions, so also did the ancient Israelites rely on their own heritage. To state this more directly with respect to the subject of this volume, religious leaders in the Jewish community have since earliest times looked to the Torah for moral guidance, and this use of their heritage has been comparable to how the Israelites themselves—i.e., the very ones who were involved in producing this Bible—appropriated the revered traditions from their own past. Jewish ethics, just as biblical ethics, is a coordination of past and present. Moral problems in any given epoch tend to be resolved through appeal to cases and values of the past, and if the new situation presents new moral problems or new dimensions to old moral problems then the resolution is reached through a creative appropriation of this moral tradition. This occurs through a dialogue with the tradition—searching for ancient indications of how to resolve the new problem while at the same time bringing contemporary ideas to bear on the way the tradition is to be understood. In the early rabbinic period the heritage was the Hebrew Bible together with oral traditions of its interpretation; for the medieval and modern periods of commentaries and responsa-literature the Mishnah-Talmud took on an authoritative role second only to that of the Bible. Yet, the interpreter in any such case introduces new perceptions and cultural values which can create—even if only to the slightest degree—a novel moral position which adds to the ever-ongoing stream of Jewish ethics. The old is infused with the new, just as the new is informed by the old.

As indicated, there is precedent for this in the growth of the biblical tradition itself. While it may appear that the learned rabbi is approaching the Bible (later also the Mishnah-Talmud) as if it were a fixed "product" in the sense described above, this moral interpreter is a participant in a "process" similar to that which brought the Bible (and the Misnah-Talmud) into existence. There may, nonetheless, seem to be a difference of some import. Prior to the canonical fixation of the biblical text, new interpretations could become incorporated into the literature, and in fact this is presumably how the literary traditions grew.[2] After canonization, however, the interpreter could not add to the biblical text itself (except perhaps through textual variants) but only to the history of its exegesis.[3] This difference, while correct in its formal sense, nonetheless does not detract from the similar dynamics which prevail in both cases of appropriation: looking to past revered tradition as a source for moral values and directives and yet also allowing new factors or perceptions and even new values to assist in interpreting—and thus changing—

the old morality because of the contemporary moral dilemmas. Typically this occurs through an effort to discover in the past the truths which may previously not have been known but which the new generation can now stipulate as having been implicit from the beginning. In both Israelite and Jewish history the process of moral socialization is complemented by creative appropriation of the past. One is born with a heritage and learns to affirm it, yet one also necessarily, though usually unknowingly, modifies this legacy in the very act of appropriating it.[4] Such a process accounts, in part, for the powerful resiliency of both biblical ethics and Jewish ethics.

A word about moral discourse is in order at this point. As usual in this context, moral discourse comprises all discussion, explicit as well as implicit, about good or right conduct, the nature of the moral agent, the nature of the moral community, and the place of principles and norms in moral judgment. Since the Bible is not intentionally designed to be a guidebook on morals or a philosophical treatise on ethics,[5] statements related to the world of morality must be sought in a vast array of different literary forms: laws, judgments, narratives, contemplative discourses, proverbs, pronouncements, disputations, parenetic speeches, prayers, songs, and more. In most of these cases the given form will have other purposes beyond that of making moral judgments or engendering moral conduct. Narratives, for example, can also entertain, instruct, record historical events, account etiologically for present-day phenomena, provide biographical information, explore existential matters, and serve other purposes. Prophetic utterances can, in addition to addressing moral problems, also interpret historical events, announce God's word, present a vision of the future, and comment on religious practices. Any given text can have multiple intentions, and by positing a moral level in it one is not thereby necessarily arguing that this is its main or only intention. Often the primary purpose of the text in question may be wide of ethics, but careful examination could reveal that a story about a revered ancestor is in fact also presenting moral conduct paradigmatically, or that a law which regulates societal structures is at the same time suggesting indirectly that human nature is such that pragmatic controls need to be exercised, or that a hymn praising God's righteousness and justice is also affirming the orderliness of the moral universe. Such levels of meaning contribute in a major way to the makeup of biblical ethics. Moral discourse occurs also in a more direct fashion through both categorical and casuistic rules. The Ten Commandments are the best known examples of the former, while the latter are prime instances of the abovementioned "process" of moral decision-making: a specific case arises which presents extenuating circumstances so that a categorical principle needs to be modified in some respect. Exodus 21:13–14 represents such a case law in relation to the categorical laws of Exodus 21:12 and 20:13. Through all such means—whether direct or indirect—moral discourse is occurring.

Much reference has been made above to moral problems. In one sense many of these dilemmas may seem to recur more noticeably throughout the history of Israel than do specific moral principles, and one can appreciate the proposal of Rudolf Unger to key the history of literature to the history of fundamental human problems. Ethical values are rarely formed and delineated in the abstract; rather, people face specific, concrete difficulties to which they must respond. Thus are values articulated and tested, always potentially different for each new generation and in each distinctive context. The following are examples of the range of areas in which ancient Israelites faced moral problems: the relationship between men and women; the relationship between adults and children; licit and illicit sexual behavior; the terms of marriage and divorce; the importance of family; the rights of the individual in relation to the rights of the community; the treatment of those who are defenseless or oppressed in society—specifically the poor, the widow, the orphan, the stranger, and the slave; the distribution of wealth; the use of money and capital, as in loans; the rights of ownership; the value of inheritance; the need for release from oppressive structures (e.g., the exodus theme and the sabbath- and Jubilee-year laws); order and security within society; the rights and obligations of leaders within government; the structure of societal governance; obligations to foreign rulers; warfare and military service; relations to non-Israelites; the administration of justice; the system of punishment and restitution; blood vengeance; truth-telling; legal commitments and contracts; hospitality; character; motives and intentions. In the face of these the Israelites developed the moral values which eventually became registered in the Hebrew Bible, and in nearly every case these values and requirements were understood to be founded in the very nature and will of God.

In sum: The ancient Israelites faced moral problems in the various areas of their life, corporately and individually. Throughout the course of their history the changing circumstances often required new moral responses to old problems as well as decisions about unfamiliar dilemmas. Their discourse about morality tended to use the forms of everyday speech rather than the language of philosophical, analytical inquiry. At most points moral decision-making relied heavily on the traditions and values of the past, but these could also be scrutinized, reinterpreted, or replaced. The Hebrew Bible incorporates into itself much of this process, even though it is also the end-product of this process and is susceptible of being used now in only its final form as a moral guide and authority. However, the gradual process by which both the literature and also the moral norms and judgments developed is equally of importance for the ethics of the Hebrew Bible, and this process can similarly constitute a precedent for the ways in which subsequent adherents to the Judeo-Christian heritage can make use of the biblical tradition.

II. THE PROBLEM

To maintain that morality is related to historical process discloses a range of substantive issues, among them: the formation or discovery or moral value within a specific but fluid cultural context, the extent to which value can reside in traditional materials or may even *be* the substance of these cultural traditions, the process of transmitting and receiving value and tradition, the roles of the community as well as individuals in constituting both values and traditions, and the reasons for continuity and discontinuity in these areas over a span of time. For our purposes here we will focus on only two issues, which can be described quite simply. For the sake of convenience we will take a cross-section of the tradition process and call one generation the predecessor and the next generation the successor. Our two problems are:

A. What interest does the predecessor have in the values and traditions of the successor? Why should one generation attempt to transmit—or even unintentionally transmit—material to the next generation? *What* is it that is being passed on, and by what means? What investment does the predecessor have in these values and traditions, and what control does this first generation have over the appropriation by the next? This issue presents us directly with the problem of historical-critical investigation, i.e., of attempting to discern the activity and intent of the predecessor when we possess only the statement that the successor has preserved for us. Stated more dramatically, why should we even be interested in the values and traditions of persons in the early periods when we possess the canonical statement of the last ones in the line?

B. What is at stake for the successor in appropriating values and traditions from the predecessor? Why should one thing be accepted, another abandoned, and a third significantly modified? How are we to understand the function of convention and the role of innovation? Does the successor generation realize that it in turn will eventually become the predecessor to a new generation, and how does this affect the formation of its own values and traditions, in short the way this generation constitutes meaning for itself in its own time?

It should be apparent in these two problems that we are purposely leaving aside questions concerning the individual agent and value, for the very existence of tradition necessarily means that more than one individual is involved. To be sure, the creative genius, functioning as pioneer or catalyst, can initiate a new course in moral thought as well as any group can; however, it is necessary for a later generation to appropriate these moral insights or norms if they are to have any effect beyond their first appearance. The focal point for us in this context thus becomes *the intersubjective community in temporal duration*. We have stated the two problems very schematically and theoretically; the process of transmission is much more complex and gradual than what we have portrayed, for generations overlap and merge into each other. There are many more than just two stages in actuality, and indeed each person or group is simultaneously both a successor of those before and a predecessor of those who follow. Furthermore, the intentions of the predecessor are, in a very real sense, at the mercy of the actions of the successor, for ultimately the future must attend to the past if the past is going to have an impact beyond itself. It will rarely be possible for us from this distance to observe one generation's acts of transmitting values and traditions to the next—even though it was continually happening, we posit, throughout the course of Israel's history. Our purpose here is to use this simplified schema as a means of highlighting the ground that moral values and literary traditions hold in common.

III. THE SUCCESSION NARRATIVE

Comprising the block of materials in 2 Samuel 9–20 and 1 Kings 1–2, the "Succession Narrative" deals with events in the later life of David and the question of who will succeed him on the throne. Since the landmark work of Leonard Rost in 1926, it has been common among most scholars to view this narrative as a unified literary whole deriving from the early monarchic period. Martin Noth (1943) concurred with this judgment, identifying only a few isolated verses (mainly in 1 Kings 2) as Deuteronomistic.[6] Indeed this narrative is commonly considered one of the earliest examples of Israelite historiography (see, for example, Gerhard von Rad), presumably in written form already in the Solomonic era, although Sigmund Mowinckel (22f.) has suggested that the exilic Deuteronomist might have had to rely on oral sources in writing the whole "Deuteronomistic saga," as he calls it, because the previous written sources were likely to have been lost in the fall of Jerusalem and the deportation. Only recently have some critics begun to question the literary integrity of the Succession Narrative, either by postulating varying stages in its early development (so Ernst Würthwein; also James Flanagan, who maintains that the bulk of this material originally formed a "court history of David," to which the texts about Solomon's succession were later added), or by finding evidence of a Deuteronomistic redaction (Timo Veijola) or even rather radical compositional work on these narrative materials by the exilic "D-group" (R. A. Carlson). For those who still dispute any such late reworking of these materials and who prefer to consider these chapters solely as the literary product of an individual or group near the time of Solomon, there has been considerable divergence in determining what might have motivated its original writing—whether it intended, e.g., to glorify Solomon (Rost: 128; similarly Tomoo Ishida, 1982), or to express national pride (Edmund Jacob: 29), or to portray YHWH's power and control over the human sphere (von Rad: 12–41), or to supply moral instruction for later generations (Morton Smith), or to meet possible threats to the stability of the Davidic dynasty (R. N. Whybray), or to underscore the importance of the wise courtier and the prophet in counseling the king (Frank Crüsemann: 180–93).

To be sure, this narrative whole may seem to be an unlikely choice as an example for our suggestions about the possible relationship between tradition and value, for this text does not appear to have undergone as long and intricate a growth as many other parts of the Hebrew Bible. However, every text is unique in some respect, and the thesis must be able to hold good over a wide range of biblical materials. The practical usefulness of the Succession Narrative for us is that we do not need to consider a limitless series of predecessors and successors, for the composition probably attained relatively fixed form very early and was not substantially reinterpreted again until the exilic period. We will thus be able to see somewhat more distinctly the role of both the predecessors' values and the successors' values in the tradition process. My comments will necessarily be quite brief on each point.

A. *The Predeccessors*

Considered first from the perspective of the *predeccessor generation*, the fundamental relationship between moral values and the growth of tradition appears especially at two points:

1) Those experiences of a people which hold an importance for their ongoing societal, political, economic, religious and moral life need to become interpreted and rendered in the form of linguistic traditions (possibly also in institutional structures) if they are to be remembered and are to have an impact on later generations. This is the process of "Sedimentation," in which the predecessors contribute to the heterogeneous "stock of knowledge" which a society or an individual possesses and which allows these people to understand and attribute meaning to their own experiences.[7] Any given predecessor generation itself has a stock of knowledge derived from its own past, and this antecedent meaning structure provides the basis for the newly sedimented layer of interpreted experience. In preserving the memory of any such event or experience, the predecessors display—explicitly or implicitly—their own moral values not only in the form of interpretations which are incorpo-

rated into the traditions but also in the very process of selecting, ordering, and preserving the materials. These values either may be embedded and indirectly communicated, or they may be more explicitly stated as norms or judgments. When the traditions have to do with social realities and institutions, the interpretations often take the form of legitimating or, on the other hand, criticizing these phenomena (Berger and Luckmann: 92ff.). The net result of this activity of sedimentation and interpretation, therefore, is to inform and socialize the successors not just concerning what they should do, but especially also about why things are as they are. In the terms of Clifford Geertz (126), there is within such a cultural system both an "ought" and an "is," and fundamentally the former is seen to grow out of the latter. The predecessors thus pass on a context for moral action, specifying the possibilities and limitations present in that community's life in the light of certain important experiences. How intentional this is in the predecessor's consciousness will vary, but such intentionality is not a necessary condition for the inevitable occurrence of this process.

So perceived, the Succession Narrative embodies values associated with national identity, political principles, the functioning of governmental leaders, the nature of a dynastic monarchy, and the relation of subject to king. To theology and ethics are given the chief interpretative roles. The predecessors who first sedimented these political experiences in narrative form were likely contemporaneous—or nearly so—with David's and Solomon's reigns, observers of the tumultuous events, rivalries, and intrigues which accompanied the onset of the dynastic line. The actual identity of these predecessors can only be speculated. It is not unlikely that they had some official position at the court, perhaps as some type of annalists; there is at least circumstantial evidence of such a position in later monarchic periods.[8] Yet they were not mere ideologues or propagandists acting at the behest of the state. While the markings normally associated with oral tradition are not as visible here as in other biblical literature, the stories themselves, with their vivid descriptions of corruption and tension in high places, are the kind which would have had great popular appeal and would likely have circulated among the people during the time of David and Solomon, and even much later after they had been rendered into a written narrative (see also D. M. Gunn). The composers of such a narrative, in other words, were probably reflecting, indeed incorporating, popular values and sentiments, not simply propounding state dogma.

Most remarkable in the Succession Narrative is a decided ambivalence in assessing David and Solomon. A common way to account for this has been to posit that the narrative was at the outset either pro-Davidic or pro-Solomonic propaganda. Würthwein even suggests that the traditions originally were very critical of both of them because the two rules established an absolute monarchy and a dynastic line rather than leaving the choice of king to the free citizens of the land. Such an attitude could underlie especially 2 Samuel 11, the story of David and Bathsheba, and also 1 Kings 1–2, the account of Solomon's elimination of rivals and threats to the throne. For Würthwein these traditions expressed old premonarchic values of tribal autonomy and egalitarian social structures. Only later were the materials reinterpreted theologically to give divine approval to the Davidic dynasty. Würthwein's suggestions are not implausible, although he seems to be underestimating some of the positive aspects in the stories that surely are mostly directed against David, maintains that this was done by Solomon's supporters in order to defend the legitimacy of Solomon's place on David's throne. Carlson also concurs in finding the anti-Davidic element the strongest in 2 Samuel 9–24, although he attributes it instead to the Deuteronomists writing from the perspectives of the exile. Veijola, on the other hand, considers the early narrative to have been in opposition to Solomon's succession to the throne, while David is generally pictured in a better light throughout the Books of Samuel (132–33). Such diverse readings of the material—and there are numerous other interpretations in the scholarly literature—are to a great extent a result of the effort to determine the primary intention of the original narrative or of its authors. Too often the intention which is posited has a monolithic character, as if there could only have been one single or dominant purpose for the narrative; indeed, this in turn often becomes used as a source-critical or redaction-critical criterion. This overlooks the multiple roles which a narrative can play. Whether the early authors sought to praise David or to legitimate Solomon or generally to revel in the existence of the new empire, moral values could very much be at play in the narrative as well. What is notable is that the predecessors included both praiseworthy and offensive behavior in this account of the momentous beginnings of the Israelite dynasty.

Rudolf Smend has stated that "the most productive periods [in the development of literary traditions] are when something is not yet self-evident or when something is no longer self-evident but is perhaps threatened by loss or even lost already" (65). This would fit equally well for the two periods when the Succession Narrative was being formed—the time near the United Monarchy when the future of the great empire and of the new dynastic line was not yet known and, much later, the period of the exile when Israel's political fate appeared dismal. In each case the respective generation sedimented its experiences in the form of literary traditions which could provide its own and later generations with the means for understanding and responding to such realities as the political institution of the monarchy. The accomplishement of the predecessors living near the time of Solomon is especially noteworthy, for they were preserving the record of Israel's initial experience with their own kings. It was a momentous shift from the social structures of the premonarchic world,[9] and the people of that generation were bound to be somewhat uncertain about its implications. Perhaps this accounts for the narrative depictions of the monarchs as alternatively devious and heroic, unjust and benevolent, manipulative and victimized, frail and powerful. The royal institution itself is not considered unequivocally good, yet also not as something which must be eliminated. Moreover, royal succession, whether along dynastic (see Tomoo Ishida, 1977), "democratic," or usurpative lines, is shown to be as intricate and complex as it can in reality be—a political process with direct implications for the people living at the time, but also an ideolgical matter pertaining to the self-understanding of the ongoing state. On moral, religious, and political levels, the narrative seeks to deal with the legitimacy of Solomon to replace David as the leader of the Israelites.[10]

2) The predecessors not only preserve and interpret experiences and phenomena for the successors; they also attempt to guide the successor generation in specific courses of action. This we tend to associate more directly with morality, although we do not always realize that such suasion can sometimes take very subtle and indirect forms. Moral guidance will only on certain occasions occur through such explicit forms as directives, laws, proverbs, or exhortation. Narratives can be extremely effective in conveying the principles of right and good which the predecessors want the succeeding generations to claim as their own. Thus traditions of various sorts become the means of inculcating and guiding those who follow.

The Succession Narrative contains no norms or directives explicitly aimed at the Israelites as a whole, yet it is replete with implicit and very effective moral judgment. Is there a more forceful description of lust and manipulation than the story of David, Bathsheba, and Uriah (2 Samuel 11)? Or again, consider the inexorable path from ambition to demise in Absalom's quest for the throne (2 Samuel 15–18). Or, observe the sickness that occasions rape, with the poignant insight about Amnon afterwards that "the hatred which he had for [Tamar] exceeded the love which he had had for her" previously (2 Samuel 13:15). Or, can one read the whole Succession Narrative without realizing by its end in 1 Kings 2 exactly what can happen to those who dare to go counter to the wishes of kings? The latter lesson remains intact whether the persons behind these stories are in favor of or are opposed to the monarchic and dynastic principle which David inaugurated.

Yet these stories also contain positive paradigms. Thus we see in dramatic form such virtues as kindness (2 Samuel 9, David's generosity to Mephibosheth and thus to Saul's line), compassion even in the face of malice (2 Samuel 18:5, David's concern for his son Absalom who has tried to usurp the throne), loyalty (2 Samuel 11, by Uriah in contrast to David's exploitation; and 2 Samuel 15:21, Ittai's Ruth-like pledge), the importance of principles (2 Samuel 10, the result of the Ammonites's disgracing David's messengers), shrewdness when facing opposition (2 Samuel 15:34, David's sending his counselor to subvert the opponent), or the rending sympathy for a misguided loved one (2 Samuel 19:1 [H], David's lament over Absalom). These are among the most effective biblical statements concerning some of the marks of the ideal moral person.

Just as powerful are the two cases which demonstrate moral reasoning. In both cases the narrator carefully develops the scene so that David convicts himself. The one is Nathan's well-known parable about the rich man's exploitation of the poor man, and the result is that David sees he has wrongly manipulated Bathsheba and Uriah to his own benefit (2 Samuel 12). The other is the intriguing interchange between David and the woman of Tekoa, as a result of which David realizes that he must bring about a reconciliation between himself and Absalom (2 Samuel 14).

Whybray and Crüsemann have suggested that the Succession Narrative stems from wisdom circles in the royal court. While their arguments are not convincing, it can nonetheless be noted that, even if they are correct, the traditions are still functioning in a directive fashion similar to what has just been described. Thus, according to them, the literature serves to guide new generations of courtiers in the proper way to counsel kings and to act in the royal court. The predecessors thus inculcate their successors in the appropriate manner of functioning in the king's presence, and thus how best to enjoy life in all its aspects.

More likely, the intent of the predecessors is to present later generations of Israelites, not just the court counselors, with these traditions about David and Solomon and to do so in a manner whereby these successors will acquire moral values while at the same time learning about their national and religious heritage. As such, the human figures in the stories become—among other things—paradigms for moral virtues to be emulated or counter-examples for vices and practices to be avoided. With such indirect narrative means the predecessors can hope to socialize morally the following generations.

B. *The Successors*

Considered from the other perspective of the *successor generation*, the relationship between value and tradition assumes again a double contour. We will be much briefer in our references to the Succession Narrative since many of the examples will be recognized from the foregoing discussions.

1) The successor generation appropriates and internalizes tradition from the predecessor in the natural and inevitable process of socialization. This may be more apparent for the individual than for a larger

group or the society as a whole, but it occurs at the latter level as well. As Berger and Luckmann describe it (129), the individual "is not born a member of society. He is born with a predisposition toward sociality, and he becomes a member of society." While the society is not simply the individual writ large, a culture does develop a character, distinctiveness, and ethos—all of these quite complex and often with divergent internal elements—which can maintain some continuity over a lengthy period of time. Thus each generation, viewed schematically, will learn from its predecessors key perspectives and values which allow the society to continue to function with a sense for its heritage yet also with an alertness to new historical situations. Tradition thus becomes constitutive, life-giving, grounding. The successor generation finds in it an identity as well as a means for interpreting and responding to the world—for "reality-maintenance," to use Berger and Luckmann's term (147ff.). Yet also a part of this is value-maintenance, insofar as these successors assign normative meaning to sedimented experiences of their predecessors.

Taking our example of the Succession Narrative, we can sense the social and religious role it must have had if it in fact was—ex hypothesi—transmitted relatively unchanged for three and one-half centuries, from the time of Solomon on down to its exilic appropriation by the Deuteronomists. It is not difficult to imagine, although we have no direct evidence to verify it, that the intervening generations of Israelites saw in this narrative a rich variety of materials and interpretations appropriate for their own response to life. As mentioned earlier, the values embodied here relate to the nature of the political structure, the national heritage and especially the national hero David, and moral standards of good and evil. For instance, a given successor generation would be able to perceive in the story of David and Bathsheba not only the power and prerogatives which adhere to the monarchic office, but also the higher moral principle of justice to which even the king, as much as everyone else, is subject. In the innocent loyalty of Uriah one sees the dutiful commitment that is owed to the king, even in the face of one's own total vulnerability. Successor generations could see in the story models for their own behavior, while the traditions could also serve to remind the monarchs of their limits and ideals. In this way institutions are legitimated, moral and political values are articulated, the communal context of living is preserved—in short, reality is maintained and managed successfully by the new generation just as it had been by their predecessors.

2) However, the successor's appropriation can also take a critical or a creative turn if the new historical situation encourages it. There are times when old values and understandings are not adequate if the new generation is to meet the demands of its own time. There are among those occasions identified by Schutz (103–32) as disturbances or interruptions of the process of sedimentation, points in which a "topically rele-

vant theme of experience" is "dropped" or "covered" because attention is shifted away from it: "Our own history is nothing else than the articulated history of our discoveries and their undoing in our autobiographically determined situation" (132). We can see this most dramatically in times of crisis or radical social change, for in such periods an unusual literary activity is likely to occur. Consider how many of the Israelite traditions either began to appear, or were developed substantially, or were rendered into written form during such nodal times as the premonarchic consolidation of the Israelites, the establishment of the monarchy, the decline and fall of first the North and then the South, the Babylonian exile, the restoration, and the Hellenistic period. If the people had not been able to adjust to the new social demands, they would likely have perished. To the adaptability of the Israelites as much as to their constancy we owe the Hebrew Bible. While tradition is constitutive and grounding, it is not simply handed over to traditionalists, to those who aim to control and limit its meaning. Not only can totally new traditions or new values be introduced in order to deal with new demands, but also it is very possible for the community instead to find a new depth of understanding in the sedimented past (see Barr: 190; also Stanley Hauerwas). For the view of life in the Israelite literary traditions is itself not simple, nor does it encourage premature or naive action, no more than does any good literature (Wellek and Warren: 36). It is addressive, inviting engagement, commitment, and creative response.

We can see this to some extent in the Succession Narrative. As indicated, the bulk of the creative formation of this text occurred very early, probably during or soon after the Davidic and Solomonic reigns when the various stories would have been recounted to describe the character of the two monarchs and also the nature of the emergent institution of the monarchy. It may be that some of this was prompted by opposition to beginning a dynasty, as Würthwein has advocated. At any rate, the next creative stage may not have occurred until the time of the Deuteronomists in the exilic period. Even then it did not experience an in-depth reworking, but a theological reinterpretation which needed to be entered by the redactors at only a few points. The narrative itself already managed more than adequately to portray the exemplary heroism of the good king as well as the pernicious temptations of power. What was not adequately articulated for this generation in exile was that YHWH had wanted the earthly monarch to rule more in keeping with the divine will and that the very continuation of the dynasty was to be understood as an indication of the divine presence in Israel. As Veijola has reconstructed the Deuteronomists' contributions,[11] not all of their additions were intended simply for the literary purposes of tying together the narrative materials in the books of Samuel and Kings through a system of foreshadowings and flashbacks. The Deuteronomists were above all theologically moved to underscore the religious, and thereby also the moral dimensions of the ideal king. Thus David is pictured as forgiving and manganimous (2 Samuel 9), as piously humble and willing to suffer for religious virtues (2 Samuel 15:25f; 16:11f.), and as law-abiding (1 Kings 2:3f.). Solomon is morally exonerated for his punitive acts against challenges to the throne; this is accomplished through several insertions which implicate the opponents themselves (1 Kings 2, passim). And above all, new additions emphasize that the dynasty is established by divine will and proclaimed to be eternal (1 Kings 2:7, 33, 45; also note especially 2 Samuel 7:8b, 11b, 13, 16, 18–21, 25–29). Thereby the catastrophe of 587 is interpreted not as the end but as the actual beginning of hope (Veijola: 137). The Succession Narrative must surely have had clear religious intentions from early times, but it fell to the Deuteronomists to develop fully the theological interpretations, as they often did elsewhere in the biblical literature. Through this means they spoke a word of encouragement to the exiled people while at the same time making their faults apparent to them. This exilic appropriation of ancient materials was designed not only to reestablish continuity with the past but also to aid that generation in dealing with the harsh new realities which they faced (see also Peter Ackroyd).

In conclusion, we should reemphasize that the Hebrew Bible was intended to be neither an ethical treatise nor a handbook of ready-made, easily accessible moral values. It has, of course, existed for two millennia as a fixed product from which people could draw rules and norms for the moral life. Yet one can also look deeper into the text and observe some of the gradual process which brought much of this literature into existence. Such literary parts will potentially be vested with the values of the many people responsible even in the remotest way for their growth, and these prior layers in the literature—just as also the very process of continual appropriation and reinterpretation—also belong to the makeup of biblical ethics. In light of the varying functions which the traditions had for the people over time, perhaps the best way to understand moral values is to relate them to the fundamental meanings which are constituted, instituted, inculcated, internalized, and reformed among the people. The traditions give people a basepoint for self-understanding and a guide for proper conduct. They relieve each new generation from the need to create a moral universe de novo. Yet old answers are not always sufficient for new moral problems. Just as the generation near the time of David and Solomon sought to come to terms with the moral implications of the new monarchy, so also did the Deuteronomists seek to cope with life in exile. In both cases they drew on their respective heritages while also creating their own new response to their circumstances. The above analysis has purposely focused on the creative work of the Davidic and Solomonic generation and the acquisitive act of the exilic people, although it is clear that both generations are in fact carrying out both roles. Endlessly, the predecessors socialize and the successors appropriate—but critically and creatively, commensurate with their needs. In this dynamic process persons search, collectively and individually, for proper moral conduct in the face of their own dilemmas and ambiguities. This is a fundamental characteristic of the moral history of the ancient Isrelites leading up to the fixed text of the Hebrew Bible—just as it is of Jewish ethics in the two millennia since that period.

NOTES

[1] An obvious and important question is whether there were limits within which these moral responses needed to remain, and what these limits were. Certainly there were many living within Israel whose moral practices did not conform to norms now evident in the Hebrew Bible. Furthermore, this question of limits is especially affected by the very diversity of moral judgments within the Hebrew Bible itself. One way to resolve the issue is to attempt to identify any fundamental values present throughout the range of the biblical literature. However, this cannot be satisfactorily determined without a comprehensive ethical analysis of the Hebrew Bible and any other literary and artifactual remains that can allow us to observe the moral life of the ancient Israelites.

[2] For a history of research into the growth of the biblical traditions, see D. Knight, 1975. On a more specific aspect of this process, Michael Fishbane (1977; 1979) demonstrates the phenomenon of inner-biblical midrash or exegesis, whereby older fixed texts could be reformulated and thus reinterpreted by writers of later biblical literature.

[3] James Barr (27–29, 162–64) refers to this distinction as "tradition before scripture" and "tradition after scripture." To be sure, the differentiation is a heuristic portrayal of what historically was a gradual and natural shift from one stage to another. Furthermore, as Edward Farley notes (9–11, 51–54), during the history of Israel itself one can at most speak only of "an incipient Scripture principle": a tradition was remembered and recited, but it was not equated with an identifiable written entity.

[4] Even the very act of affirming a tradition from the past without seemingly changing it does in fact constitute an alteration of it since this adds to the tradition a new layer of effect, another stratum in its history.

[5] The terms "ethics" and "morality" (and their adjectives and adverbs) are often used interchangeably. In this essay, however, they will be distinguished according to the convention followed by some ethicists: "Morality" designates the actual realm of human conduct according to principles of good or right, while "ethics" refers primarily to the philosophical or theological inquiry of the good and the right and the capacity of humans to act morally. In this sense, the Hebrew Bible records all manner of moral actions and judgments, but it is hardly an ethical analysis such as is to be expected within the discipline of ethics. See James M. Gustafson (85–97) for a discussion of this distinction and for an overview of some of the classic issues of ethics. Note also Henry David Aiken's more nuanced distinction concerning four main levels of moral discourse: expressive-evocative, moral, ethical, and post-ethical (64–87).

[6] Subsequently, in his commentary (1968:8–11), Noth considered 1 Kings 2 to be a series of "Nachträge" to the rest of the Succession Narrative.

[7] This concept of sedimentation is drawn from Alfred Schutz: 75ff., 103ff.; as well as Peter L. Berger and Thomas Luckmann: 67ff. See also Howard L. Harrod's discussion which ties it more directly to ethics, and Edward Farley's incorporation of it into theological method.

[8] For more discussion of this and other administrative offices in the king's court, see

Tryggve Mettinger (1971) and G. W. Ahlström. Much of the evidence must necessarily come from what can be learned about state government in Egypt and elsewhere in the ancient Near East.

[9] This transition from the premonarchic to the monarchic era in ancient Israel involved a wide range of significant historical factors. Reliable knowledge about this period has long been elusive, and there is an increasing interest among current scholars to probe for more evidences and to reconsider old interpretations. (For discussion of some of the issues, see Hayim Tadmor; and Baruch Halpern.) In this essay we can do no more than note that these developments in the social, economic, political and religious spheres of that time had a crucial impact on the group that we are here calling the "predecessors." These persons lived through these historical events, or were told of them by their elders who had experienced them. They were shaped by these happenings, and in turn helped to shape them as they interpreted them for others. In other words, our "predecessors" were themselves the "successors" of their own past, just as the exilic generation later became the successors of this people living during the time of the United Kingdom. For the purpose of our argument here, however, we will focus only on the predecessor role of the generation in the Davidic or Solomonic period.

[10] Tryggve Mettinger (1976) offers a helpful analysis of this problem of the legitimation of kings in ancient Israel and neighboring countries.

[11] Veijola (see especially 13–14 and 127–42 for discussion and bibliographical references) finds most appropriate the hypothesis of a three-stage redaction by the exilic Deuteronomists: first the main one with basically historical interests (DtrG), followed by a second under prophetic influence (DtrP), and finally a third with a legal orientation (DtrN). Such a multiplicity of editorial reworkings of the Succession Narrative only strengthens our thesis that the successor generations needed to engage the traditional materials with new structures of meaning and values.

RESPONSE TO DOUGLAS KNIGHT
BUT *HOW* DOES IT HAPPEN? A NOTE ON "PREDECESSORS AND SUCCESSORS"

Lou H. Silberman
The University of Arizona

The proposal or, rather, the proposals offered by Douglas Knight are deserving of close attention, beginning with his suggestion that the alternative approaches to Scriptures he describes as a source of ethical insight are at opposite ends of a continuum. He is certainly correct as he views these positions from the vantage point of a contemporary biblical scholar, but it is evident from the reading not of scholarly literature but the daily press that not all share his irenic view that those who see the Hebrew Bible (and the Greek New Testament as well) as not "product" but "entity," "fixed, final and . . . authoritative," are merely at the other end of his continuum. "A high administration official," to use the unsavory euphemism foisted upon the public by the venal media, seems to think that, to quote Knight: "Moral values . . . inhere in it as objective realities, ascertainable through careful study of the text without reference to the multiple social realities which might have produced these value statements." All one need do is thump the "Book" and proclaim that the answers to the questions of complex urban technological society in the declining years of the twentieth century are here. There is a midrashic colloquy between God and Abraham in which the former chides the latter: "You want to hold on to both ends of the rope." What was not possible for him is not possible for us.

Left with the "development process" Knight turns to the problem with which such a position confronts someone who is yet convinced that although the Hebrew Bible does not offer push-button answers, it is nonetheless a potent source of insight into, understanding of and even solutions or clues to solutions of those ineluctable questions confronting contemporary society. Here he offers a particularly meaningful and helpful pattern in his analysis of the process by means of which value is transmitted. His portrayal of the "tradition process" in terms of "predecessors" and "successors" sets the inner life of Scriptures in sharp focus but it does more than that as it illuminates our role as successors. If we are able to grasp the dynamic of the predecessor-successor process in Scriptures we may, at the same time, be enabled to learn how we as successors receive or may receive what the generations of predecessors—here again we face the continuing process in which Scriptures are appropriated in ever new contexts—have transmitted to us.

The choice of the "Succession Narrative" to exhibit this action is itself interesting. One would think that an examination of the way in which legal ideas moved out of their pre-Israelite contexts into an emerging Israelite context and what happened to them in that context would have been the way to go. For example, one thinks of the background of the "Hebrew Slave" material in Exodus 21; of the added nuance in Deuteronomy 15, 15: "You shall remember that you were a slave in the land of Egypt; therefore I command you this day"; and of the existential application in Jeremiah 34, 8–16. (See, too, its continuing echo in Nehemiah 5,5.) Yet by choosing a more intricate structure, Knight did himself and us a good turn, for he demonstrates that the movement of values can and does take place at a deeper and more subtle level than ordinarily anticipated. The double discussion of 1) the Predecessors' preservation of an interpretation of experiences and phenomena for their successors and their concern "to guide the successor generation in specific courses of action," and 2) the internalization of appropriation of tradition by the successors and the critical or creative turn that appropriation may take "if the new historical situation encourages it"; that double discussion is a valuable contribution to our further understanding of the inner workings of Scripture. We recognize that this indeed is what may have taken place. What, however, is missing, what could move that "may" closer to a more positive affirmation, is *how* this transmission and interaction is accomplished. What is called for is an analysis of the rhetorical moves of the predecessors, intended to presuade and to convict the successors, and parallel analysis of the response mechanisms by and through which the predecessors' intentions—are in large or small measure fulfilled in the successors.

A paradigmatic case is indeed to be found within the Succession Narrative in the Story of David, Bathsheba and Uriah to which Knight refers. In it, it seems evident, the confrontations of David by Nathan and most particularly Nathan's parable, may well have had a wider intention than the immediate situation. In a forthcoming value of *Semeia Studies (Text and Reality: Aspects of Reference in Biblical Texts* by Bernard C. Lategan and Willem S. Vorster) the authors examine and debate the way or ways in which the parable may have convicted David. It is then the "how" of that "may" I am calling for. Without it, in this case as in others, we may recognize that the literary tradition does provide the means by which the predecessors forward to the successors their experiences and their concerns in the hope or in the expectation that these will inform the latter's ethical behavior, but we shall not understand how this happened and thus be deprived, as predecessors, of ways of continuing the process.

As a postscript let me add a warning. The predecessors' intentions may be of no avail! The ethical values preserved and sent forward may, despite rhetorical excellence, be unheard, partially heard or misheard. Again the case in point is the episode noted. When one goes in search of the re-echoing of the ethical judgment in Nathan's parable in Rabbinic literature, one is hard put to hear any such. The transformation of the role of David, in much of that literature, into a pious scholar has filtered out the dissonances of this and other questionable episodes in his life. The rabbinic readings of this episode summarized on pages 103–104 of *Louis Ginzberg's Legends of the Jews, IV* and the notes thereto on pages 264–266 of volume VI make it clear that the successors often do not hear what the predecessors are saying. That, too, may be our problem or our fate.

TO SPEAK, HOW TO SPEAK, AND WHEN NOT TO SPEAK: ANSWERS FROM EARLY RABBINIC STORIES

Joel Gereboff
Arizona State University

ABSTRACT

This essay examines how early rabbinic documents embody moral precepts. The methodological starting point is Sol Roth's emphasis on role-modelling as an important tool for nuturing moral development. Both Mishnah and Tosefta—the earliest documents of rabbinic Judaism—present many stories or conversations which portray the rabbis acting in certain ways. Here we examine stories that throw light on a particular theme: the proper use of speech. Through a study of how their heroes use speech, we adduce the implicit values of the rabbinic redactors. For this story, Mishnah and Tosefta are studied separately. The wisdom of this choice appears as we find that the two documents have different theories as to the character of proper speech. Mishnah wants speech to be used to achieve reconciliation. Tosefta sees proper speech as that which confronts and corrects. These studies shows us how moral values are passed on through narrative discourse.

The recent comments by Sol Roth on the Jewish methodology for solving social problems stress the importance Judaism places on role modeling for moral development. Roth states:

> Fundamentally two approaches to the solution of social problems are possible. One is sociological. Society's social structure can be transformed in such a way that the impact of specific problems may be reduced or even eradicated. This might be done by the restructuring of old institutions or the introduction of new ones. The other is moral. Alternatively, the individual member of society, through a process of education, may undergo changes in character which could also lead to the same result. . . . Greater emphasis is placed by Judaism on the building of moral character than on the creation of new institutional forms. Judaism's definition in terms of commandments means that even the realization of the social objective is ultimately dependent on the development of moral character. (150–51, 155)

Roth goes on to note how the combined efforts of the school and the family contribute to moral development. He remarks:

> One important consequence of Judaism's emphasis on the practical form of education is that the family becomes the crucial instrument in the process that leads to the cultivation of the sense of morality and the development of a commitment to the moral principles. The burden of education does not belong exclusively to the school. It must be carried by the family as well, in the Jewish view, must even assume the greater share. The school will fulfill the purpose of communication of knowledge and provide the explanation, even the justification, of principles. But the practice of precepts must be prompted and supervised in the home and by parents. . . . It is necessary that children be taught to practice the precepts of conduct into which the principle of respect is translated and which have the capacity to instill the attitude of respect into the hearts of the young. When children are trained to avoid sitting on a seat reserved for a parent, to refrain from contradicting parents, never to respond to a parent with abuse, they learn, in practice, the sense of reverence that constitutes respect for a parent. (151–52)

Roth's claim that for successful moral development children and their parents must observe the moral precepts is quite accurate. Roth, however, draws too sharp of a contrast between parents and teachers; for teachers, and the people they teach about, also provide role models for children. When teachers act in certain ways, when they tell stories about authoritative personalities, or when they relate narratives found in normative or sacred texts, they provide the students with data that may greatly shape their moral characters. In this paper we discuss the moral values conveyed by the actions of individuals in stories[1] in the two earliest rabbinic documents, Mishnah (edited *circa* 200 C.E.) and Tosefta (edited *circa* 250 C.E.).

The redactors of Mishnah and Tosefta have included most narratives because of their relevance to the legal concerns of their redactional contexts. Most of the accounts, moreover on their own, focus upon legal issues. As a result, only a small number of narratives in Mishnah and Tosefta describe what can be called "moral actions."[2] These few accounts, furthermore, focus upon a number of different moral matters, with only one or two sources pertaining to each issue. It, therefore, would be inappropriate to reconstruct the ideas of Mishnah and Tosefta on these issues based on such meager evidence. Several narratives, however, explicitly deal with the same theme, the proper use of human speech. Since many of the other narratives, and all of the debates, contain discourse, we shall examine all of them. This large body of data allows us to describe the various views of Mishnah and Tosefta on the most common interpersonal activity of rabbinic society. What rabbis and students of Torah do most is talk. Through the stories they relate, the composers of rabbinic literature provide role models indicating the proper conduct of this action.[3]

We separately examine the materials in Mishnah and Tosefta. Recent work on rabbinic literature stresses the importance of a documentary approach.[4] One should not homogenize diverse ideas from different rabbinic documents and create an artificial composite entitled "the rabbinic view of x." We shall emphasize the accounts in Mishnah and then, for purposes of comparison, introduce the reports in Tosefta. In our discussions of the narratives we concentrate upon their literary structure, as well as their substance. Meaning comes from form, not just from content. We pay particular attention to the syntagmatic structure of the narratives, to word plays in them and to the formulaic features of their rhetoric.

i

The narrator of the first account that we examine from Mishnah locates a key difference between rabbis and ignorant people in their employment of speech. This story thus indicates the importance given to the question of the nature of proper speech.

A. He who slaps the ear (htwq‘) of his fellow gives him [for compensation for embarrassment] a *sela*.
B. R. Judah says in the name of R. Yose the Galilean, "A *maneh*."
C. He slapped him (strw), he gives him two hundred *zuz*.
D. With the back of his hand, he gives him four hundred *zuz*.
E. He mutilated (srm) his ear, plucked out his hair, spit and his spit touched him, pulled his cloak off of him, loosened the hair of a woman in the market [C, N, K, P, Pr, Pc lack: in the market], he gives four hundred *zuz*.
F. This is the general rule [C, N, K, P, Pr, Pc lack: this is the general rule]: All [assessments are made] in accordance with his [a person's] honor.
G. Said R. Aquiba, "Even poor ones in Israel, they look upon them as if they are freemen who have lost their possessions.
H. "For they are children of Abraham, Isaac, and Jacob."
I. M‘SH B: One who loosened the hair of a woman in the market [C, N, K, P, Pr, Pc lack: in the market].
J. She came before R. Aquiba,
K. and he obligated him [the one who committed the act] to pay her four hundred *zuz*.
L. He [the guilty party] said to him, "Rabbi, give me some time."

M. And he gave him time.
N. He observed her standing by the entry to her yard, and he broke before her a cruse, and in it was about an *issar* of oil.
O. She uncovered her head, scoped up [the oil] with her hands, and placed her hand on her head.
P. He had set up witnesses [to observe] her.
Q. And he came before R. Aquiba.
R. He said to him, "Rabbi, to this one I should give four hundred *zuz*"?
S. He said to him, "You have said nothing.
T. "For he that wounds himself,
U. "even though he is not permitted [to do so],
V. "he is exempt
W. "And others who wound him, they are liable.
X. "And he who cuts down his plantings,
Y. "even though he is not permitted,
Z. "he is exempt.
AA. "And others who cut down his plantings, they are liable."

M.B.Q. 8:6

The story consists of four scenes: 1) the initial act in the market, I; 2) the first appearance before Aquiba, J-K + L-M; 3) the trick played by the convicted man, N-P; 4) the second appearance before Aquiba, Q-R + S-AA. The narrator tells the first part of the story almost entirely through descriptive sentences. In the opening sections only the man speaks at L. He also talks first in the final scene, at R. The silence of Aquiba then is dramatically reversed at S. Aquiba's initial comment reinforces the picture created by the narrator; he tells the man, "you have said nothing." Aquiba then proceeds to state the correct lesson. The utilization of a law in standard legal form at V-AA, instead of a simple descriptive remark, "and R. Aquiba obligated him to pay," dramatically brings to the surface the rabbinical role of a judge who is an authoritative teacher. The rabbi, who is reticent to start, knows how to reveal effectively his knowledge; he knows how to speak. The man who wants to expose the woman ends up revealing his own poor character and ignorance of the law. P further underscores his last point. The man thought he was clever and well-versed in the law and, accordingly, set up the required witnesses. But his efforts were for naught since his entire plan was misconceived. In the end, the man looks like a fool, the woman degrades herself (O), and the witnesses are duped. Only Aquiba emerges as a positive figure.

The above analysis accounts for a curious omission in the story. Nowhere in the narrative does the storyteller have Aquiba say, as a remark attributed to him at G-H does, that the woman should receive the compensation because she, like all Israelites, are children of Abraham, Isaac, and Jacob. This claim could have been appended to K, if the latter had read, "Said R. Aquiba,'You must pay her four hundred zuz, for even she is a child of Abraham, Isaac, and Jacob.'" The failure to include this statement in D-G allows the narrator to avoid portraying her, at any point, in a positive light. The sage is the sole individual who conducts himself properly and who knows how to use his words correctly.

The following three separate accounts also deal with the effects of the words of different kinds of people. In the first story a common person, through his statements, foils his own well designed plans. Because of their use of language two different sages, in the second and third reports, are able to bring events to positive conclusions.

A. He who sanctifies his field [that he inherited] when the Jubilee is not [in force]—
B. They say to him, "You declare first [how much you wish to pay for the redemption of the field." Since when the Jubilee is not in force the field is redeemed at market value, and not at the fixed rate of fifty *sheqels* per *homer* of land, an auction must be held]
C. For the owner pays an added fifth.
D. But no other man pays the added fifth
E. M'SH B: One man sanctified his field because of its poor quality.
F. They said to him, "You declare (pth) first."
G. He said, "Lo, it is mine for an *issar.*
H. Said R. Yose, "This one said,'Only for [the value of] an egg.'"
I. "For what is sanctified is redeemed by money or by something worth money."
J. They said to him, "It is yours."
K. He turned out to lose an *issar*, and his field was before him [still his].

M. Arakh. 8:1

A. A woman suffered five miscarriages that were in doubt, five issues that were in doubt, she brings one sacrifice, and she eats from animal offerings, and the remainder [of the sacrifices] is not incumbent upon her.
B. [If she suffered] five miscarriages, five certain issues, she brings one sacrifice, and eats from animal offerings, and the remainder is incumbent upon her.
C. M'SH Š: A pair of birds (qynym) in Jerusalem [went up in price and] stood at a gold *denar* [twenty-five silver *denars*].
D. Said R. Simeon b. Gamaliel, "By this sanctuary (hm'wn hzh), I shall not rest tonight until they shall be at [silver] *denars.*"
E. And he entered the *bet din,* and taught that:

F. [If] she suffered five certain miscarriages, five certain issues, she brings one sacrifice, and eats from animal offerings, and the remainder is not incumbent upon her.
G. And the pairs of birds stood on that day at one-quarter *denar* [each].

M. Kerit, 1:7

A. If there is a wound [covered by a scab] on her [a woman who has found a bloodstain on herself], and it can open again and bleed, lo, she can blame it [the bloodstain] on that [wound].
B. M'SH B: One woman who came before R. Aquiba.
C. She said to him, "I have seen a bloodstain."
D. He said to her, "Perhaps there was a wound on you"?
E. She said to him, "Yes, but it has healed."
F. [He said to her,] "Perhaps it can open and bleed"?
G. She said to him, "Yes."
H. And R. Aquiba declared her clean.
I. His disciples did he see staring at one another.
J. He said to them, "Why is this matter hard in your eyes? For the sages stated the rule not to produce a strict ruling, but to produce a lenient ruling.
K. "as it is said, *And if a woman have an issue and her issue in her flesh be blood [Lev. 15:19]*—
L. "not a stain but blood."

M. Nid. 8:2–3

The common person in M. Arakh. 8:1, wishing to be rid of his field of poor quality, dedicated it to the Temple. But because of the procedure used to insure that the Temple receives money, and not land, the person ended up owning the field and losing money. The speech of the person, ignorant of the law, causes him double losses. By contrast, Simeon b. Gamaliel in M. Kerit. 1:7 and Aquiba in M. Nid. 8:2-2 use their words for constructive purposes. Concerned that the price of birds needed for sacrifices had become prohibitive, Simeon b. Gamaliel threatened to filibuster in the court and to call for a change in the law until they became cheaper. To accomplish this goal he was willing to change the number of required sacrifices. The story underscores his sensitivity to the plight of the poor, as well as his verbal skills.[5] Aquiba in M. Nid. 8: 2-3 plays the role of the sagacious judge who knows how to frame inquiries in order to arrive at correct decisions. He conducts careful and meticulous investigations conforming to the spirit of the law. In addition to rendering the proper ruling, Aquiba knows how to instruct students. He is cognizant of their reactions and precedes his formulation of the reasons for his decision (J-L) with an appropriate question that articulates their perceptions and thoughts. The three above stories, along with the first one we analyzed, M. B.Q. 8:6, show that proper speech is the mark of a wise person. The correct use of language is instructive and beneficial. On the other hand, improper and inopportune remarks have detrimental results.

Knowing how to speak also includes knowing when it is best not to say anything. The next accounts are the two mishnaic narratives that center upon the idea of silence. In one, a sage refused to disclose the teachings of a colleague. In the other account, a priest wished to reveal information that should have been kept secret.

A. ["An important general rule have they said concerning the Seventh Year: Whatever is gathered solely as food for man may not be used as an emollient for men . . . or cattle; and whatever is not solely for food for man may be used as an emollient for man, but not for cattle; and whatever is not solely either for food for man or for food for cattle—if he intended it for food for man and for food for cattle, they place on it the stringent rules regarding man and cattle. . . ." (M. Sheb.-8:1)].
B. . A hide which one has anointed with oil for the Seventh Year—
C. R. Eliezer says, "It is to be burned."
D. And sages say, "He should eat [produce of] equal value (y'kl kngdw)."
E. They said before R. Aquiba, "R. Eliezer used to say, 'A hide which one has anointed with oil of the Seventh Year—it is to be burned.'"
F. He said to them, "Silence. I shall not say to you what R. Eliezer says concerning it."

M. Sheb. 8:9

A. Further, they said before him, "R. Eliezer used to say, 'He who eats the bread of Samaritans is like him who eats the flesh of a pig.'"
B. He said to them, "Silence. I shall not tell you what R. Eliezer says concerning it."

M. Sheb. 8: 10

A. Thirteen *shofar* [shaped chests for donations], thirteen tables, thirteen places for prostrations were in the Temple.
B. Those of the house of Rabban Gamaliel and Hananiah the Prefect of the Priests used to prostrate themselves fourteen [times].
C. And where was the extra [place]?
D. Opposite the storage bin for the wood.
E. For they had a tradition from their fathers that the ark was hidden away there [at the time of the destruction of the First Temple, see 2 Chr. 35:3].
F. M'SH B: One priest who was occupied (mt'śq) [therein],
G. and he saw that [a piece of the] floor was lower than the rest.

H. He came and told his fellow [priests].
I. He did not have sufficient (hśpq) [time] to finish his remark before his soul departed.
J. And they knew assuredly (byḥwd) that the ark was hidden away there.

M. Sheb. 6:1–2

In the two identically reports, M. Sheb. 8:9E-F, Sheb. 8:10, Aquiba strongly reacts to the students' remarks and suppresses the teachings of Eliezer. Neither of the reasons for this response, nor the exact rulings of Eliezer are clear. But it is certain that, according to Aquiba, Eliezer's views are more lenient than those attributed to him by the anonymous "they."[6] According to Aquiba, Eliezer in Sheb. 8:9 either agrees with the opinion of sages, D, or holds the even more lenient position that the hide may be used without paying any fine or redemption fee. In the case of Sheb. 8:10, Eliezer's opinion may be that one may eat Samaritan bread. We can only speculate why Aquiba would not want to transmit whichever of these possible notions are the real ideas of Eliezer. Perhaps Aquiba did not want Eliezer to come across as a lenient judge, or perhaps he did not want anyone to know that any sage held a most liberal view. In spite of these uncertainties, these stories do show clearly that at times silence is an appropriate action. Without knowing the motivations for Aquiba's alleged response, we cannot generalize regarding the proper use of silence.

M. Sheq. 6:1–2 does not leave us with the above uncertainties. In this instance the reason for suppressing information is clear: the hiding place of the ark should not become public knowledge among the priesthood. This well crafted story indicates that a discerning priest will garner this information and keep it to himself (J). The narrator reinforces this message through the literary features of this unit. F-J is somewhat atypical for mishnaic narratives in its complete avoidance of discourse. Remarks could have been assigned to the individual single priest at H and to the group of priests at J. The narrator also creates suspense by not revealing, until the conclusion of the account, the identity of the location noticed by the priest. The reader realizes from D that the information gained by the priest is of great significance and potentially dangerous. But the reason this knowledge is threatening is not cited until J. The secrecy is maintained even at the end of the story, for it nowhere reveals the exact location of the hidden ark.

The crucial word in J, *yḥwd*, with its double meaning of "assuredly" and "individually" conveys the notion that discerning priests know how to treat the information they acquire. Each priest kept his discovery to himself and did not make it a topic of conversation. A play on words in F and I also underscores the theme of this unit. F. describes the priest by the infrequently used term, mt'sq, "occupied." The use of this term yields the lesson that the priest, who should have kept to his business, did not, and as a result, he never had the opportunity, *hspq*, to finish stating his ideas. The implication is that sticking to one's affairs, and not talking about inappropriate matters, allows a person to finish his or her tasks.

The few accounts we have just examined concern themselves to some degree with aspects of the proper use of speech. The majority of the narratives, debates and dialogues in Mishnah do not center upon this matter. Nevertheless, the way in which they portray interpersonal communications provides insight into mishnaic views on speaking. The rhetorical features of the sayings and discussions in these materials suggest that people should address each other straightforwardly, respond directly to questions and avoid harsh criticisms and *ad hominem* attacks. In most accounts people either simply state their opinions, ask their questions, advance arguments justifying their views or reject the positions of others by showing their logical flaws, their detrimental results, their opposition to established facts or their lack of support from an authoritative document.[7] The items in Mishnah containing discourse indicate that discussants must have an opportunity to state their cases without interruption. Conversations should be based upon mutual respect. People should not vilify others for asking poor questions or for putting forward weak or unfounded ideas. They also need not defer to their superiors in learning or office. Thus in no mishnaic sources does a person request permission from someone else to speak. In only four narratives (Ber. 2:5, Pes. 6:2, Ned. 9:5, Bekh. 4:4) people refer to the titles of the person they address. In all four cases a party questions the views of another person, and we shall return to these reports in our comments upon mishnaic opinions on offering criticisms and correction. Debates in Mishnah similarly omit all reference to titles. Discussions focus upon the issues. Personalities and statuses are irrelevant considerations.

In the course of interpersonal communications people often have to correct one another. They also often have the opportunity to relate uncomplimentary incidents. From the mishnaic accounts under analysis we can reconstruct the views of the redactors of Mishnah on the manner for correcting people and on the propriety of transmitting negative reports. Mishnah omits almost all reports that reflect poorly upon people. It also contains only a small number of sources in which people castigate others. These silences suggest that according to Mishnah one should not discuss the negative aspects of people. In all of Mishnah only nine reports seem to depict unfavorably individuals or groups.[8] Even in these accounts, especially those that are brief, people simply state the pertinent facts without adding an evaluative commentary about the person under scrutiny. For example, in M. Suk. 2:7 the House of Hillel simply relate to the House of Shammai tht the elders of the latter group once did not correct one of their members who was following Hillelite practices. The House of Hillel do not add anything to the details of the report. They do not even state that the House of Shammai were inconsistent.[9] Facts are allowed to speak for themselves, and the reader must deduce that the people acted incorrectly. Similarly, when people note an error in the recollections, opinions, exegeses or arguments of others, they just describe the mistake and do not accentuate the grievousness of the fault or the stupidity of the person. Only five narratives (Suk. 2:7, Ket. 8:1, Ned. 5:6, Naz. 7:4, Makhs. 3:4) and five debates and discussions (Ber. 1:3, Pes. 6:2, B.B. 9:10, Nid. 6:14, Yad. 4:6-7) contain rebukes or explicit statements that the person has erred. Not even all of these ten items contain remarks that actually attack a person. In five cases (Suk 2:7, Naz. 7:4, Makhs. 3:4, Nid. 6:14, Yad. 4:6-7) one party simply states explicitly that the other has erred. As noted, Mishnah generally just records responses without adding introductory comments specifying that the person has made a mistake. The statements of masters in two of the five remaining reports, Ket. 8:1 and B.B. 9:10, are expressions of frustration, not of anger. Through these remarks these sages indirectly note the weaknesses of their own views. The three remaining pericopae, Ber. 1:3, Pes. 6:2, Ned. 5:6, are the sole harshly critical statements in Mishnah. People familiar with all of Mishnah would undoubtedly conclude that they should use their words only to correct or question and not to rebuke or speak unkindly of others.

Three fairly lengthy stories in Mishnah detail tensions of pre- and post-70 C.E. eras. M.R.H. 2:8–9 records an incident pointing to strife between the Patriarch Gamaliel and rabbis; Ta. 3:8 is an uncomplimentary story about the miracle worker, Honi; Ed. 5:6–7 suggests that the pre-70 figure Aqabyah was excommunicated because of his refusal to retract three opinions opposing majority views. All of these accounts about controversies, however, end with a reconciliation of the conflicting parties. Speech serves as the means for achieving this resolution of tensions. The reports against Honi (Ta. 3:8), which through its narrative indicates that he was not totally successful in having God respond to his rain-inducing rites, end with a comment by the pre-70 prototypical rabbi, Simeon b. Shetah, that criticizes Honi and, at the same time, accords him the status of a member of the group of sages.[10] In a similar vein, the critical account about Aqabyah, Ed. 5:6–7, concludes with that figure advising his son to reconcile himself with the majority of the sages. The narrator allows Aqabyah to explain his recommendations. Aqabyah bases his counsel on important rabbinic principles, and he also does not contradict his own actions. A remark by Aqabyah at the beginning of the account further tones down its negative force, for according to that comment Aqabyah claims that he persisted in holding to his opinions in order that he could not be accused of retracting for self-interested motives. Finally, the overall redactor of the unit includes a comment by a sage that disputes the claim that Aqabyah was ever excommunicated. The speeches by Aqabyah and by this sage thus smooth over the noted tensions. An examination of the report about Gamaliel's harsh tretment of Joshua, R.H. 2:8–9, will show that this narrative also concludes on a note of reconciliation. This account is as follows:

A. Rabban Gamaliel had pictures of the shapes of the moon on a tablet and on the wall of his upper room, which he used to show to the untrained people (hdywtwt) and say, "Did you see it in this way or in that?"

B. 1. M'SH Š: Two came and said, "We saw it in the east in the morning and in the east in the evening."
   2. Said R. Yohanan b. Nury, "They are false witnesses."
   3. When they came to Yavneh,
   4. Rabban Gamaliel accepted [their evidence].

C. 1. Again, two came and said, "We saw at its expected time, yet in the night of the added day it did not appear."
   2. And Rabban Gamaliel accepted [their evidence].
   3. Said R. Dosa b. Harkinas, "They are false witnesses: how can they testify about a woman that she has given birth if the next day her belly is between her teeth"?
   4. Said to him R. Joshua, "I approve your words (rw'h 'ny 't dbryk)."

D. Rabban Gamaliel sent him [a message], "I charge you to come to me, with your staff and your money, on the Day of Atonement as it falls according to your reckoning."

E. 1. R. Aqiba went [to R. Joshua] and found him troubled.
   2. He said to him, "I am able to learn that whatever Rabban Gamaliel has done is done,
   3. "for it is written, *These are the set feasts of the Holy Lord, holy convocations, which you shall proclaim* [Lev. 23:4].
   4. "Whether in their time or whether not in their time, I have no other *set feasts* but these."

F. 1. [R. Joshua] went (b' lw) to R. Dosa b. Harkinas.
   2 He said to him, "If we come to judge [the decisions of] the court of Rabban Gamaliel, we shall have to judge [the decisions of] every court which has arisen from the days of Moses until now.
   3. For it is written, *Then went up Moses and Aaron, Nadav and Abihu, and seventy of the elders of Israel* [Ex. 24:9].
   4. "And why are the names of the elders not spelled out (ntpršw)? Rather, it is to teach that any three [judges] who arise as a court over Israel are like the court of Moses."

G. He took his staff and his money in his hand, and went to Yavneh to

Rabban Gamaliel on the day which fell as the Day of Atonement according to his reckoning.

H. Rabban Gamaliel stood up and kissed him on his head.

I. He said to him, "Come in peace, my master and my disciple: my master in wisdom, and my disciple, in that you have accepted [K, P, C.: upon yourself; N: upon himself] my words."

M. R.H. 2:8–9

Even this most critical report, which has a Patriarch command a sage to violate the most sacred day of the Jewish calendar, ends in compromise.[11] Through his words of peace in I, Gamaliel overcomes his harsh order of D. In addition to its explicit claim that Gamaliel comes to terms with Joshua, Gamaliel's speech subtly makes him take on the characteristics of a rabbi. I is the only point in the narrative where, like the various rabbis throughout the account, Gamaliel explains his rulings and statements. Until I, the storyteller simply records Gamaliel's decisions and commands. By playing on the double meaning of the term "words" (C4 vs. I), the narrator brings out the conflict between Patriarchal rule by fiat and rabbinic rule by reason and exegesis. From the perspective of the Patriarch, the authority of his court rests on the office and person of the Patriarch. Patriarchs need not give their reasons for their rulings. Rabbinic decisions, on the other hand, are correct because of the quality of the arguments supporting them. Good arguments convince Joshua that he should accept the Patriarch's decree, and he does just this. But the Patriarch, through his own words, at I, indicates that also he needs to explain his actions. Consistent with the impression left by the rest of Mishnah, this account, and the other two lengthy narratives, imply that humans should use their ability to speak to bring people together, not to create disharmony among them. Harmony does not, however, mean agreement. People may differ on matters. But their remarks should not be phrased so as to make future conversations difficult or impossible.[12]

We now turn to one final aspect of Mishnah's use of speech. The claim that silence is an important value for the redactors of Mishnah and therefore that the silences of that work are important indicators of its concerns may explain its only limited reference to biblical figures. Consistent with the general lack of citation of biblical verses as prooftexts for its claims, Mishnah uses as precedents only a small number of narratives that detail the actions of biblical figures.[13] These few items sharply contrast with the numerous reports about rabbinic figures that serve as precedents for mishnaic assertions. A remark in one of the stories about a biblical personality, M. Qid. 4:14, may provide insight into these redactional preferences. According to this text, "Abraham, our father, performed the whole Torah before it was given." This remark, with its description of Abraham as "our father" and with its specification of "the whole Torah," gives the impression that a strong continuity exists between Abraham and the heroes of Mishnah, the rabbis. Rabbis are like biblical figures, and as a result, the readers of Mishnah could not conceive that the actions of rabbis oppose those of biblical personalities. This remark establishes the continuity of the biblical and rabbinic figures, but it and the few other remarks about early Israelite figures, do not cause the latter personalities to overshadow the importance and authority of rabbinic masters. Rabbis, and not biblical individuals, are central to Mishnah, and they provide role models for other Jews. The redactors have achieved this effect by their careful use of speech, particularly by their purposeful silences.

ii

The narratives, discussions and debates in Tosefta generate a more complex set of opinions than Mishnah regarding the use of speech. The nature of the discourse contained in most of these sources is similar to that in Mishnah. People generally state their views without adding extraneous comments, raise straightforward questions or advance arguments unencumbered by derogatory remarks.[14] Tosefta also contains several accounts that indicate that silence is at times an acceptable response.[15] While Tosefta in these ways continues the mishnaic patterns of rhetoric, it augments Mishnah on one aspect of the use of speech and differs with that earlier rabbinic document on three others. Several accounts in Tosefta revolve around the correctness of using evasive or false language. Mishnaic sources provide no information on this matter. Tosefta first differs from Mishnah regarding the appropriateness of relating uncomplimentary stories and of strongly criticizing people. A person exposed to Tosefta would conclude that one may make harsh comments and retell negative reports. The inclusion of a number of accounts in which people defer to their superiors is consistent with this view found in Tosefta that speech can be utilized to highlight differences between individuals. This is the second area of divergence between the two documents. Speech in Mishnah brings people together; in Tosefta it sometimes divides them. Tosefta finally diverges from Mishnah by recording more stories about biblical characters. Our ensuing remarks take up these alternative views of Tosefta.

In four accounts in Tosefta (Suk. 1:8–9, Yeb. 3, Hul. 2:24, Hag. 2:11–12) masters respond to questions in indirect ways. The narrators of the first three incidents treat these answers as appropriate replies. The sage who uses such tactics in the fourth report is condemned. We first present the three accounts that positively evaluate circumlocution.

A. A large courtyard surrounded by pillars, lo, the pillars are like sides [for a Sukkah].
B. One may make its fellow [pillar into a] side so that he may drink and sleep.
C. And moreover, one may stand up a bed [on a festival] and spread a sheet over it so that the sunlight does not come in either on those who eat or on a dead [body].
D. Sages admit to R. Eliezer that they do not make tents to begin with on the festival, and there is no need to say [that they do not do so on the Sabbath]."
E. 1. [E, Lon., ed. prin. add: About what did they disagree? About adding (to a tent); for R. Eliezer says, "They do not add (to a tent) on the festival, and there is no need to say (anything about) the Sabbath."]
  2. And sages say, "They add [to an already existent tent] on the Sabbath, and there is no need to say [anything] about the festival." [D-E = Tos. Shab. 12:14]
F. M'SH B: Eliezer was sitting in the Sukkah of R. Yohanan b. Ilai in Caesarea,
G. and [E, Lon. lack: and] the sun came into (hgych) the Sukkah.
H. He [Yohanan] said to him, "What is [the law] about spreading a sheet over it?
I. He said to him, "You have no tribe in Israel [E, Lon., ed. prin. lack: in Israel] that did not put forth (h'myd) a prophet [E, Lon.: a judge].
J. The sun reached the middle of the Sukkah.
K. He said to him, "What is [the law] about spreading a sheet over it"?
L. He said to him, "You have no tribe that did not put forth a judge [E, Lon.: a prophet].
M. "The tribe of Judah and Benjamin put forth kings according to the instruction of prophets."
N. The sun reached the feet of R. Eliezer.
O. He [Yohanan] took the sheet and spread it over the Sukkah.
P. And R. Eliezer stretched out his feet (hpšyl) and went away.

Tos. Suk. 1:8–9

A. They asked R. Eliezer, "A *mamzer*—may he inherit?
He said to them, "may he perform *halisah*."
B. "May he perform *halisah*"
He said to them, "May he inherit"?
C. "May he inherit"?
He said to them, "May one plaster his house"?
D. [Should be: "May one plaster his house"?]
He said to them, "May one plaster his grave"?

E. "May one plaster his grave"?
   He said to them, "May one raise dogs"?
F. "May one raise dogs"?
   He said to them, "May one raise pigs"?
G. "May one raise pigs"?
   He said, "May one raise roosters"?
H. "May one raise roosters"?
   He said to them, "May one raise small cattle"?
I. "May one raise small cattle"?
   He said to them, "May one save the shepherd from the wolf"?
J. "May one save the shepherd from the wolf"?
   He said to them, "It seems you have asked me only concerning the (kbśh) lamb"?
K. And as regards the lamb, "May one save [it]"?
   He said to them, "It seems you have asked only about the shepherd."
L. "So-and-so, what is he as to [does he enter] the world to come?
   So and so, what is he as to the world to come"?
   He said to them, "It seems that you have asked only about so-and-so."
M. "And so-and-so, what is he [= his status] as to the world to come"?
N. R. Eliezer was not putting them off, but he never said anything which he had not heard.

Tos. Yeb. 3

A. 1. MʻSH B: R. Eliezer who was seized on account of matter of *minut* [heresy],
   2. and they brought him up before the court (bmh) for judgment.
B. That *hegemon* said to him, "Should an elder like you involve [himself] in these matters"?
C. He said to him, "The judge is faithful for me (n'mn dyn 'ly)." [= "I rely upon the Judge."]
D. That *hegemon* thought that he spoke only of him [himself], but he meant only his Father who is in heaven.
E. He said to him, "Since you have relied upon me, so have I said, 'Is it possible that these white hairs should err (hsybwt hllw tw'ym) in such matters'? *Dimissus* [= Pardoned (dymwś)]. Lo, you are free."

Tos. Hul. 2:24

Eliezer for three different reasons does not directly answer the questions posed to him in these three narratives. In the case of Tos. Suk. 1:8–9 the narrator does not supply Eliezer's motivation for not telling R. Yohanan that it is wrong to spread a sheet over the *sukkah*. One, however, can deduce from the failure of Eliezer to correct Yohanan, after the latter had spread out the sheet (O-P), that Eliezer did not wish to tell his host that the latter's actions were incorrect. Now the nature of Eliezer's response here opposes that of his and other sages' replies in other narratives. He and other rabbis correct colleagues elsewhere when they err. We, therefore, cannot determine from this evidence when it is appropriate not to answer a question directly so as not to embarrass or correct someone. The reasons for Eliezer's course of action in the other two accounts are clear. The author of Tos. Yeb., in N, gives Eliezer's motivation: Eliezer did not want to offer an opinion on a subject about which he received no tradition. The narrator, however, does not explain why Eliezer did not simply state that he had not heard any teaching on the matter. In a number of accounts in Mishnah and Tosefta (M. Bekh. 6:8, Kerit. 3:7–9, Neg. 7:4, 11:7, Par. 1:1,3, Tos. Ed. 1:6, Bekh 4:15, Neg. 6:1, Nid. 1:5) he and other masters reply in just this way. Eliezer in Tos. Hul. 2:24 employs a third type of evasive reply for dealing with a difficult situation. Here he uses a double *entendre* (C) to outwit the gentile judge. The *hegemon's* own comments in E further highlight the contrast between the wise Israelite sage's use of speech and the stupidity of the locution of the foreign judge. The latter misunderstands Eliezer and, in E, also ironically and unknowingly mischaracterizes himself and Eliezer. This report suggests that it is appropriate for an Israelite to use misleading language to extract himself from a dangerous situation involving non-Jews.

Eliezer in none of these reports actually lies. These accounts indicate only that, at times, it is permissible to answer questions in a non-direct manner. A story in Tos. Hag. 2:11–12, involving Hillel, shows that one should not tell falsehoods. This account contrasts the actions and statements of Hillel with those of a Shammaite, Baba b. Buta, and it reads as follows:

A.1. M'SH B: Hillel the Elder [b. Bes. 20a: who brought his whole offering to lay hands on it] who laid hands on the whole offering in the courtyard.
    2. and [E, Lon. lack: and] the disciplines of [E, Lon., ed. prin.: House of] Shammai collected against him.
B. He said to them, "Come and see that she is a female, and I do prepare it [as] peace offerings."
C.1. He put them off (hyplygn) with words,
    2. and they [E adds: went out] went their way.
D. Immediately, the hands of the House of Shammai became strengthened, and they sought to establish the law according to them [E, Lon.: according to their words].
E. And there was there Baba b. Buta,
F. who was of the disciples of the House of Shammai and knew that the

law in all places [E, Lon. lack: in all places] is according to the House of Hillel.
G. He went and brought all the *sheep of Qedar*, and set them up in the courtyard, and said to them, "Whoever needs to bring whole offerings and to bring peace offerings let him come and take and lay on hands."
H. They came and took the beasts and offered up whole offerings [Lon.: and peace offerings], and laid hands on them.
I. On that day the law was established according to the words of the House of Hillel, and no one protested the matter.

Tos. Hag. 2:11–12

A-I is a unitary account, which as Jonah Frankel (146–49) has argued, is a fictional story created to teach the lesson that a person's actions must overtly conform to his/her thoughts and values. Success depends upon living up to this standard. The failure to carry out one's view, even in the face of pressure, yields negative results. Hillel succumbed to the threat of the crowd, tried to deceive them, and as a result, his actions almost led to the supremacy of the House of Shammai. By contrast, the Shammaite Baba b. Buta acts in a straightforward manner and does what he knows is right, even in the face of the opposition of his colleagues. Just as Baba claims should be the case, the law, accordingly, is established in agreement with the opinion of the House of Hillel. A closer look at the literary traits and substantive background of A-I will support these assertions.

The story draws upon the Houses' dispute in M. Hag. 2:3. That passage reads:

A. 1. The House of Shammai say, "They bring peace offerings [which may be either male or female animals, on a festival day] and do not lay hands thereon,
2. "but [they do] not [bring] whole offerings [which are only males]."
B. The House of Hillel say, "They bring [both] peace offerings and whole offerings, and they lay their hands thereon."

In light of the above opinions, the only thing Hillel can do in B, if he wants the Shammaites to believe that he follows their view, is to claim that his offering is a female, a peace offering. If he claimed that it was a male, then the Shammaites could still think that his sacrifice was a whole offering. Now while Hillel's response should have satisfied the Shammaites with regard to their view about the kind of sacrifices one offers on a festival, they still should have objected to Hillel because he laid his hands on the animal. The Shammaites thus seem to know that

Hillel really did not act in conformmity with their view. They, however, are quite happy not to challenge Hillel further, for he had already caved in to their pressure. The storyteller in the first section, A-D, of the narrative, A-I depicts both Hillel and the House of Shammai as people who do not completely stand up for their convictions. Hillel lies to the Shammaites, and they overlook part of his actions. In the end, neither Hillel nor the Shammaites succeed in having matters follow their views. D and E-I make it perfectly clear that the Shammaites *sought* to establish the law in accordance with their opinion, but did not accomplish this. Only Baba b. Buta, who is consistent in thought, statement and deed, realizes his goals.

The storyteller has set up his neat contrast between Hillel and Baba by dividing the account, through the repetition of language at D and I, into two portions. A chart listing the parallel sections of A–D and E–I demonstrates the artistry of the narrator.

A-D
1. Hillel lays hands on his whole offering in the courtyard, and the Shammaites collect against him.

E-I
1. There was Baba b. Buta, a disciple of the House of Shammai, and he knew the law is in accordance with the House of Hillel's opinion. He went and brought all the sheep of Qedar and set them up in the courtyard.

2. He said to them, "Come and see if it is a peace offering."

2. And he said to them, "Whoever needs to bring whole offerings or peace offerings let him come and lay hands on it.

3. He put them off with words, and they went on their way.

3. They came and took the beasts and offered them up as whole offerings and laid hands thereon.

4. Immediately the hands of the House of Shammai became strengthened, and they sought to establish the law according to their words.

4. On that day the law was established according to the words of the House of Hillel, and no one protested the matter.

In section 1 both Hillel and Baba, under pressure, conform actions in conformity with their convictions. At 2 both individuals must explicate the meaning of the deeds in 1. Hillel tells the people *to come* and see that the animal is a peace offering. Baba tells them *to come* and take the animals and lay hands thereon and offer them as either whole or peace offerings. Because Hillel avoided a Shammaite attack by deceiving them with his *words*, not with his deeds, which as I have argued above, they knew were not in agreement with their view, the Shammaites sought to establish the law according to their *words*. By contrast, when Baba's actions and words are consistent, he succeeded in having the law established in accordance with the *words* of the House of Hillel. At that point no one *said* or *did* anything else; no one protested the matter. They used their ability to speak correctly by not saying anything.

Having examined the issue addressed solely by Tosefta, we now turn to the three matters about which it and Mishnah differ. Mishnah, as we have noted, downplays conflict. It contains only a few uncomplimentary stories and a very small number of dialogues with highly critical retorts. By contrast, the editors of Tosefta include numerous narratives that reflect poorly upon people[16] and many dialogues with harsh remarks.[17] Accordingly, readers of the two sources would develop different views regarding the correctness of speaking in these ways. Nearly seventy pericopae in Tosefta are uncomplimentary narratives or accounts with highly critical sayings. A fair number of these reports (thirteen) have parallels in Mishnah that omit these negative elements.[18] In these cases, Tosefta, in its role as a commentary to Mishnah, modifies the latter by accentuating conflicts ignored by the earlier work. The redactors of Tosefta clearly differ from their mishnaic counterparts regarding the propriety of discussing such matters.

There is a pattern to the kind of actions for which people are condemned in the accounts of Tosefta. About one-half of these items speak negatively about groups whose views oppose the positions of rabbis or their predecessors. Nine anti-priestly,[19] eight anti-Saducean,[20] eight anti-Shammaite,[21] five anti-Patriarchal[22] and three anti-heretic *(minim)*[23] reports compromise this collection of materials. In most of these instances people are criticized just for adhering to the views of these groups. The presence of these units of tradition in Tosefta indicates that its redactors maintain that one need not suppress uncomplimentary reports about one's opponents. One may rebuke a person who engages in practices in accordance with the views of a group whose opinions are incorrect. Some of these reports also criticize the followers of these groups for specific failings. These people are inconsistent, insensitive to the feelings of others and ungrateful. Failings of these sorts warrant strong condemnation.

Rabbis criticize each other or tell uncomplimentary reports about one another in twenty-six accounts.[24] Individuals are rebuked for either acting contrary to the view of the majority or using their minds poorly. In the latter instances rabbis commit serious errors of reasoning, offer poor arguments, pose inappropriate questions or fail to remember traditions. Because Tosefta contains numerous reports in which rabbis are not castigated for similar failings, we cannot generalize regarding the views of the editors of Tosefta concerning the use of harsh speech in such situations. But they clearly do not advocate its total avoidance.

By including in Tosefta negative reports and debates with harsh remarks the redactors of that work leave the impression that one should not avoid making comments that may lead to tensions within the people of Israel. Divisions exist and they need not be downplayed. The use of titles (master/student), relational terms (father, son, brother) and personal names in nearly forty remarks in Tosefta similarly accentuates differences between people.[25] Furthermore, in several of these accounts, people explicitly seek permission from another person to speak.[26] All of these accounts create the impression that society is not a homogeneous, undifferentiated mass of equals. Hierarchical relationships exist and should not be overlooked. The narratives and dialogues combining these terms, that leads to distancing people from each other, suggest that when individuals address people other than their peers they should underscore their unequal statuses. Speech, in this way as well, serves as a crucial device for restating and reinforcing the structures of the society.

Tosefta differs from Mishnah also with regard to its more frequent citation of incidents involving biblical characters.[27] This predilection is consistent with Tosefta's general tendency to comment upon Mishnah by citing biblical verses in support of claims in that earlier document. Several of the reports in Tosefta, found in chapter three of the tractate Sotah, are relevant to the issue of this paper.[28] This section of Sot. cites a series of biblical cases to illustrate the theological proposition that God repays people in kind. In three cases the narrator records the alleged corresponding speeches of God and humans. These sources maintain that the respective arrogant comments of the generation of the flood, of the inhabitants of Sodom and Nebuchadnezzar precipitated a reply in which God stated that a punishment fitting the sin would be forthcoming. Through these materials the redactors of Tosefta indicate that wrongful speech by itself is sufficient cause to warrant retribution. People must use their gift of speech with care.

iii

This investigation has yielded mixed results, and we will explore briefly the implications of this outcome for the use of rabbinic sources for the purposes of reconstructing rabbinic views on ethical matters. We have reached firm conclusions only on some points. Our discussion shows clearly that the editors of both Mishnah and Tosefta are concerned about the proper use of speech. Both works contain stories that pertain to this topic. These documents also include anonymous and assigned sayings, which we have not examined, that address this concern. Our analysis conclusively yields a second finding: the editors of Mishnah and Tosefta have different views on several matters relating to the issue at hand. These divergencies reinforce our opening methodological position that historical studies of rabbinic materials cannot ignore the documentary divisions of that large corpus of writings. One can no longer talk about "the rabbinic view of x," for much recent scholarship has shown that the compilers and authors of different rabbinic works hold divergent opinions.

While we have reached firm conclusions on the above matters, we could not generalize regarding such issues as when one should not reply to a question and when one should speak harshly and negatively. It is once again the traits of the documents in which the individual units of tradition, we have examined, appear that inhibited our efforts. The editors of Mishnah and Tosefta often ignore the original meanings of the narratives they cite and utilize them in relation to other matters. The reports generally serve in these two earliest rabbinic documents as illustrations and precedents for legal assertions, and as a result, their non-legal themes are not permitted to the issues of their redactional settings. No effort has been made to smooth over inconsistencies and unclarities resulting from the divergent and conflicting conceptions implicit within these narratives. For example, because the editors did not systematically attempt to work out a position on the manner for voicing criticism, they include narratives that together report different treatments of people under similar or identical circumstances. The inconclusiveness of some of our findings underscores the idea that limited results may follow from research that does not pay sufficient attention to the organization structure of individual rabbinic documents. The assertion that each rabbinic document has its own agendum, however, should not preclude research that seeks to uncover something other than the central purpose and message of each work. The nature of the composition of these texts, in many instances, may make it impossible to extract the view of a particular rabbinic document on a specific issue. Our study shows that even with these limitations there is much to be learned from these documents about the ethics of rabbinic Judaism.

NOTES

[1] We examine also debates and dialogues lacking even all narrative elements but the attributive formula "x said to y." Because this paper focuses upon rabbinic views on the use of speech, it is appropriate to analyze accounts that relate alleged conversations between rabbis.

[2] In addition to the materials discussed here the following stories in Mishnah provide information about rabbinic ethical views: M. Bes. 3:8, Yoma 2:2; 3:9–10, R.H. 2:5, Ned. 9:10, Git. 4:2,7, B.B. 7:1. Accounts in Tosefta with moral import include: Ber. 4:16–18, Peah 3:8;

4:10,11,18, Kil. 3:5, Kip. 1:21–22; 2:5–7; 4:2, Yeb. 6:7, Ket. 4:9; 5:9, Nez. 5:1, Git. 7:1–5, B.Q. 8:15–16, Hor. 2:5, Kel. B.B. 2:4, Ah. 4:2, Par. 3:6.

[3] We are not suggesting that the thrust of all these reports is to discuss the nature of proper speech. Our point is that these accounts implicitly take positions on this matter. A reader of the relevant materials could construct an image of the person who correctly employs speech.

[4] For a detailed discussion of this matter see, Neusner (1981:1–24) and Green (1983).

[5] Neusner (1971:I,377) notes that this story also is a polemic against the priesthood.

[6] I follow the analyses of Neusner (1973:41–43) and Newman (177).

[7] Sayings in the following stories in Mishnah have these features: Peah 2:6, Ter. 4:13, Kil. 6:4;7:5, Orl. 2:12, Shab. 16:7; 22:3, Erub. 1:2; 4:2; 6:2, Pes. 7:2, Suk. 2:1,5, Bes. 2:2,5, R.H. 1:6, Ta. 3:9, Yeb. 16:7, Ket. 2:9, Ned. 9:5,10, Nez. 5:4, Git. 7:5, Qid. 2:7, B.Q. 4:2, B.M. 4:3; 8:8, B.B. 10:8, A.Z. 1:4; 2:5; 3:4,7; 4:7,10; 6:8,9, Kerit. 3:7–10, Kel. 25:4, Neg. 7:4; 9:3; 11:7; 14:3, Nid. 8:2–3, Makhs. 3:4, Yad. 3:1; 4:3. The following debates exhibit these standard rhetorical features: Peah 5:2; 6:6; 7:7, Kil. 3:7; 5:1; 7:2, Ter. 5:4; 8:11, M.S. 2:2; 3:2, 10, Hal. 2:5, Shab. 8:7, Erub. 2:3; 3:6; 5:9; 8:7, Pes. 1:7; 6:5, Sheq. 2:4, Suk. 3:8, Bes. 1:6; 2:6, R.H. 4:1,5, Ta. 1:1, Meg. 3:1, Yeb. 7:3; 8:3; 12:3; 13:1; 14:1; 15:1; 16:7, Ket. 2:9; 4:2, Ned. 4:3; 10:6, Naz. 5:3; 6:6; 7:1; 8:1; 9:5, Git. 1:6, B.Q. 2:5; 3:9; 5:4; B.M. 3:2,7; 4:9; 10:6, Sanh. 2:2,3; 3:5,8,12; 6:2,4; 7:2,3; 9:3; 10:2,3, Mak. 1:6; 3:2,9, Shebu. 1:4,5; 3:1,5,6; 5:4; 7:5, Ed. 1:12.14; 5:6; 6:2–3, A.Z. 1:1; 2:7; 3:3,9, Hor. 1:2, Zeb. 1:1;7:4,6;8:3, 10, 12; 13:2, Men. 2:1;4:3;5:1;11:5;12:4,5, Hul. 2:7; 4:4;7:7, Bekh. 3:1; 9:8, Tem. 1:1,3,5;7:6, Kerit. 1:6;3:1,4,6,9,10; 5:2–3, Meil. 1:2, Mid. 2:2, Kel. 8:1; 25:4, Ohal. 1:3;2:7; 5:3, Neg. 10:1,2,9; 13:10, Par. 1:1, Miq. 3:3, Nid. 4:6, Makhs. 1:4; 6:8, Yad. 3:1,2;4:3,4.

[8] Three (R.H. 2:8–9, Ta, 3:8, Ed. 5:6–7) are long accounts, and we discuss them below. The six brief reports are: Ber. 2:5–7, Sheq. 1:4, Yoma 3:11, Suk. 2:7, R.H. 1:7, Naz. 1:7. These reports pertain to different groups and individuals. There is no sustained polemic against a particular party. Ber. 2:5–7 accuses the Patriarch Gamaliel of acting more stringently than his own view. The negative tone of the report is diminished by the assignment of a reply to Gamaliel. In Sheq. 1:4 Yohanan b Zakkai states that the priests expounded certain biblical texts to their own advantage. Yoma 3:11 claims that some priestly families did not teach others their cultic skills. According to a report by Yose in R.H. 1:7 a court acted differently from priests regarding the testimony of an individual. Naz. 1:7 relates that a person who was a Nazarite for a long period died upon the completion of his vow.

[9] The pericope also contains a rebuttal by the House of Shammai that disputes the Hillelite report.

[10] I follow here Green's (1979) detailed analysis of this account.

[11] Green (1981) and Kanter offer full literary and historical discussions of this narrative.

[12] The overall intent of Mishnah to create an impression of a society in perfect order probably accounts for the omissions from that work of narratives and discourse that accentuates social tensions. (See Neuser [1981] for a statement of the purposes of Mishnah.) Although it is this factor that explains the lack of polemical materials in Mishnah, a traditional member of rabbinic culture, who would not appeal to such an historical explanation, could deduce that these omissions indicate a rabbinic preference for avoiding highly critical comments.

[13] M. R.H. 3:8, Ned. 3:11, Qid. 4:14, Sot. 1:8–9; 5:5, Sanh. 2:4; 6:2, Abot 1:2; 5:3,17,18,19.

[14] Narratives with these features are: Ber. 4:12, 16–18, Peah 3:2, Demai 4:13; 5:22, Ter. 1:15, Kil. 1:3,4;3:5;4:7, Ma. 2:1, M.S. 1:13,14; 5:9, Hal. 1:6,10, Shab. 4:13; 12:12;13:14;15:8,9, Erub. 6:25, Pis. 1:10; 2:15–16;3:11;10:10, Kip. 1:16;2:5–7, Suk. 2:3, Y.T. 3:8, Ta. 2:13, Hag. 2:1,13, Yeb. 3:3; 6:7;12:11; 13:5; 14:9–10, Ket. 4:7,9;5:1, Nez. 5:2, Sot. 7:9–12; 8:6;11:18; 13:8, Git. 1:3,5;5:4, Qid. 5:5, B.Q. 7:2; 8:12,15–16; 10:12, B.M. 3:11, B.B. 2:10, Shebu. 3:6, A.Z. 1:20; 3:6; 6:7; 7:4,6,9, Zeb. 1:5;2:17, Bekh. 2:11–12, Kel. B.Q. 4:17, Kel. B.M. 1:5; 2:1–2, Kel. B.B. 1:2–3; 2:2,3; 5:6, Ah. 4:2; 5:8; 16:11–12; 18:18, Neg. 1:11; 2:3; 8:2,6; 9:9, Par. 3:6; 4:9; 10:2,3, Nid. 1:9; 4:3–4; 5:15,16–17; 6:6, Toh. 6:17, Zab. 1:5, Yad. 2:16,17, T.Y. 2:8. Debates exhibiting these

features are: Ber. 1:10; 2:13, Peah 3:6, Demai 2:2; 7:10; 8:5,7, Ter. 1:1,4; 2:13; 3:13, 16,18,19; 4:14; 5:15; 6:5; 7:2,12; 9:1, Shab. 1:5; 4:4; 5:4; 8:7, Kil. 3:16; 5:6, M.S. 1:14; 2:7,11,17,Hal. 1:7,10, Bik. 1:7, Shab. 1:20–21; 5:11–12; 8:5; 9:8; 15:9, Erub. 1:13; 2:11; 4:1; 5:24; 6:26; 7:14, Pis. 1:10; 2:19; 3:7,18; 4:2,5,6,9,12; 5:1,8; 6:2; 8:10; 10:9, Sheq. 2:8; 3:13, Kip. 1:8; 2:12, Suk. 1:1,7; 2:9, 10, Y.T. 1:5–7, 12,13, R.H. 2:10, Ta. 1:1,4; 2:7, Meg. 2:4,8; 3:28, Hag. 2:10, Yeb. 4:5, Ket. 1:6; 6:3; 8:5; 11:1, Sot. 1:2, Git. 1:5, B.Q. 3:3, B.M. 4:2, B.B. 6:1,23, Sanh. 2:8; 4:1,6; 9:11;11:7;12:3; 14:3, Ed. 1:6,14,15, A.Z. 3:13, 19; 8:6, Zeb. 1:1,5,6; 2:16; 4:1–3; 5:2,6,7:16–20; 14:3; 8:23, 11:17; 12:7, Hul. 4:3–4; 6:1–3; 7:8, Men. 1:10; 2:16; 6:19–20; 7:20; 8:19; 10:9,11,12; 11:6; 12:8–9, Bekh. 5:6–7, Arakh. 2:9, Tem. 1:17, Kerit. 1:9; 2:1, 12–13,14, Kel. B.M. 2:9; 6:11, Kel. B.Q. 6:3, Kel. B.B. 2:1–2, Ah. 1:3; 2:6,7,8; 3:2–3,7; 4:2,13–14; 15:9, Neg. 1:1; 2:3; 3:7–8,9; 7:9; 8:6,9, Par. 1:1; 2:1; 3:6; 4:9; 9:2; 10:3; 12:12, Nid. 1:9; 2:8,9; 4:13,17; 5:6,11; 7:4–5; 8:5; 9:12,13,19, Miq. 1:16–20; 3:14; 6:3; 7:11, Toh. 2:1; 3:1,8; 4:2,11; 5:15,16; 6:17; 9:12, Makhs. 1:3; 2:11,14, Zab. 1:1,5–6, Yad. 2:14,17–18, T.Y. 1:8–9; 2:9, Uqs. 1:8; 3:1–2.

[15] M.Q. 2:14–16.

[16] Ber. 1:4; 4:15; 5:2, Kil. 1:4, M.S. 3:17–18, Shab. 1:17; 13:14, Erub. 1:2, Pis, 4:13, Kip. 1:4,8,12,21–22; 2:8,10; 3:20; 4:2, Suk. 2:3; 3:1,16, Y.T. 2:6, 12, R.H. 1:15; 2:17, Ta. 2:5, Meg. 4:34, Hag. 2:6, 11–12; 3:33,35, Yeb. 10:3, Ket. 5:1,9, Sot. 13:7–8,10, B.Q. 8:13, Sanh. 6:6; 9:5, Ed. 3:3, Hul. 2:21–23,24, Kel. B.Q. 1:6, Ah. 16:2–3; 18:18, Par. 3:3, 7–8, Nid. 5:3, 16–17, Miq. 6:2–3.

[17] M.S. 4:7, Sheq. 1:7, R.H. 2:17, Yeb. 8:7, Ned. 6:5, Zeb. 1:8, Hul. 2:9, Kel. B.Q. 1:6, Ah. 3:7; 4:2; 5:11, Nid. 1:5, Miq. 7:11, Makhs. 3:3, Yad. 2:20, Uqs. 3:1,13.

[18] Ber. 4:15, Shab. 1:17, Erub. 1:2, Kip. 1:12, Y.T. 2:12, Ta. 2:5, Meg. 4:34, Sanh. 6:6; 9:5, Ed. 3:3, Hul. 2:9, Bekh. 4:8, Nid. 1:5.

[19] Pis. 4:13, Kip. 1:4,8,12,21–22; 2:8; 3:20, Sot. 3:7–8, 10.

[20] Suk. 3:1,16, Kip. 1:8, R.H. 1:15, Hag. 3:35, Par. 3:7–8, Nid. 5:3, Yad. 2:20.

[21] Shab. 1:17, Suk. 2:3, Kip. 1:4; 4:2, R.H. 2:17, Y.T. 2:16, Hag. 2:11–12, Ah. 5:11.

[22] Ber. 4:15; 5:2, Y.T. 2:12,16, Miq. 6:2–3.

[23] Kip. 2:10, Hul. 2:24, Par. 3:3.

[24] Ber. 1:4, M.S. 4:7, Sheq. 1:7, Suk. 2:1, Y.T. 2:6, Ta. 2:5, Hag. 2:6, Yeb. 8:7, Ket. 5:1, Ned. 6:5, B.Q. 8:13, Sanh. 6:6, Ed. 3:3, Zeb. 1:8, Hul. 2:9, 21–22, Bekh. 4:8, Kel. B.Q. 1:6; Ah. 3:7; 4:2; 16:2–3; 18:18, Nid. 1:5, Miq. 7:11, Makhs. 3:3, Uqs. 3:13.

[25] Ber. 1:4; 4:15, 16–18; 5:2, Peah 3:6,8,20, Demai 4:13, M.S. 5:16, Shab. 12:12, Pis. 3:20, Suk. 2:1, R.H. 2:17, Hag. 2:6, Yeb. 6:7; 14:5,9–10, Ned. 6:5, Nez. 4:7, Sot. 7:9–12; 15:11–12, Git. 1:3, Qid. 5:5, Shebu. 3:4, Zeb. 2:17, Hul. 2:21–23, 24, Kel. B.Q. 1:6, Kel. B.B. 1:2–3, Ah. 3:7; Neg. 8:2,6, Par. 3:7–8; 10:2, Nid. 10:3, Miq. 1:16–19, Yad. 2:16.

[26] Hag. 2:1, Sot. 7:9–12, Hul. 2:24, Miq. 7:11, Yad. 2:16.

[27] Ber. 4:16–18; 7:23, Kip. 2:1, R.H. 2:3, Ta. 2:1; 4:2, Sot. 3:6–4:17; 6:6; 9:3–11:5, Qid. 5:17–21, Sanh. 2:9, 10; 4:6–11, 14:4, Mak. 3:1.

[28] For example, chapter five of M. Abot contains several comments on the proper use of speech.

RESPONSE TO JOEL GEREBOFF
WHEN SPEECH IS NO SPEECH:
THE PROBLEM OF EARLY RABBINIC
RHETORIC AS DISCOURSE

Jack N. Lightstone
Concordia University

The discourse portrayed in Mishnaic and Toseftan stories functions, according to Professor Gereboff, as a model for communication among rabbinic sages and between the rabbi and the common folk. These narratives are said to convey specific norms for discourse about legally appropriate behavior. Mishnah, for example, via these stories indicates that the sages ought to "address one another straightforwardly, respond directly to questions avoid harsh criticisms and *ad hominem* attacks". Gereboff's other claims about the meaning of discourse in Mishnaic stories are of the same vein.

Gereboff, quite rightly deals separately with Toseftan evidence. But the type of conclusions differ little. Most of the implied norms Tosefta shares with Mishnah; on others, according to Gereboff, Mishnah and Tosefta part company. Some few norms appear idiomatically Toseftan.

One must laud his caution in not assimilating Toseftan and Mishnaic evidence. However, since I shall not address his interpretation of specific pericopae, but rather query his methodology in general, I shall largely restrict my remarks to his treatment of Mishnaic evidence; one may take my analyses to hold, with some qualifications, for Tosefta as well.

My claim, simply put, is that Gereboff's use of Mishnaic evidence fails to take seriously the degree to which the content of Mishnah is couched in forms and formulary patterns. This highly formalized language of Mishnah is in evidence not only in unattributed legal statements and in dispute and debates bearing attributions to named rabbis, but also in much of the putative discourse of Mishnaic stories. In other words, the Mishnaic story-precedent, itself a form introduced by the formulary uses for its actors' dialogues the same language in which almost all of Mishnah is formulated. The rhetoric of Mishnah's disputes can (1) reflect no real speech (Neusner, 1981; Green, 1979), and (2) cannot be taken to have been intended as a model for real speech of real people. The same holds for the discourse of Mishnah's stories, insofar as their discourse displays the same formalized traits as disputes, debates and anonymous statements.

A further look at M. R.H. 2:8FF, a pericope adduced by Gereboff, will help illustrate these claims and occasion their elaboration.

A. Rabban Gamaliel had pictures of the shapes of the moon on a tablet and on the wall of his upper room, which he used to show to untrained people and say, "Did you see it in this way or in that"?

B. 1. Two came and said, "We saw it in the East in the morning and in the west in the evening."
2. Said R. Yohanan b. Nuri, "They are false witnesses."
3. When they came to Yavneh,
4. Rabban Gamaliel accepted them [as true witnesses].

C. 1. Again, two came and said, "We saw it at the expected time," yet in the night of the additional day it did not appear,
2. and Rabban Gamaliel accepted them.
3. Said R. Dosa b. Harkinas, "They are false witnesses.
4. "How can they testify that a woman has given birth, and the next day her belly is between her teeth"?
5. Said to him R. Joshua, "I approve your words."

(based on Gereboff's trans.)

The putative story in B and C show remarkably little in the way of narrative features. The circumstances (B.1 and C.1) that engender response by the rabbis simply define two legal problems. In both substance and form the direct speech at B.2 and C.3 are apodases to the antecedent legal problems. Gamaliel's responses (B.4 and C.2) to the two situations resemble commonplace rulings in which operative verbs rather than lemmas provide a sage's view. In other words, the dramatic context of the story and the actions and statements attributed to rabbinic figures are all couched in the same language in evidence throughout Mishnah's other legal pericopae. I shall not argue that several standard Mishnaic disputes lie behind this part of the story; I maintain only that the language of the narrative so well reflects the forms and formularies found elsewhere in Mishnah, that one could easily construct two disputes out of B and C. Thus:

1. [If] two came and said, "We saw it in the east in the morning and in the west in the evening,"
2. R. Yohanan b. Nuri says, "They are false witnesses,"
3. and Rabban Gamaliel accepts them.

Again:

> i. [If] two came and said, "We saw it at its expected time, yet in the night of the added day it did not appear,"
> ii. R. Dosa b. Harkinas says, "They are false witnesses,"
> iii. and Rabban Gamaliel accepts them.
> iv. Said R. Joshua, "I approve the words of R. Dosa b. Harkinas."

Here we have what would pass as two typical Mishnaic disputes. They use the language, virtually unchanged, of the story. Gamaliel's acceptance of witnesses in each case is expressed in participial form, rather than in the perfect tense. The attributional formulae typical of Mishnaic debates I have changed to those found in disputes. Even the gloss at iv. attributed to Joshua is commonplace in Mishnah.

In other narratives cited by Gereboff rabbinic dialogue reflects not Mishnaic disputes, but rather simple declarative, legal statements typical of Mishnah's unattributed materials. So M. B.Q. 8:6, S-AA (trans. Gereboff):

> S. He [Aqiva] said to him, "You have said nothing.
> T. "For he that wounds himself,
> U. "even though he is not permitted [to do so],
> V. "he is exempt.
> W. And others who wound him, they are liable.
> X. "And he who cuts down his plantings,
> Y. "even though he is not permitted,
> Z. "he is exempt.
> AA. "And others who cut down his plantings, they are liable."

Gereboff himself here draws attention to the statement's form. But of its formal traits he makes the following comment: "The utilization of a law in standard legal [Mishnaic] form at V-AA . . . dramatically brings to the surface the rabbinical role of a judge who is an authoritative teacher". I see quite other ramifications to the rhetorical features of this and other exemplars. Namely, one must interpret the significance of direct speech in narratives in the context of the more salient, general features of Mishnah's language.

The editors of Mishnah have imposed upon their materials a surprisingly limited number of forms and formulary patterns (Neusner, 1981). What is more, Mishnah's rhetorical patterns have a clipped, truncated character. Concise stichs and pericopae are organized paratactically (Green, 1983). Relations of subject to predicate and to modifying clauses appear borne by this parataxis, because of the truncated nature of the language. In pericopae bearing the names of rabbis, such as disputes, one or another standard attributional formula interposes between stichs. Thus "He who . . . shall . . ." becomes [Concerning] him who . . . , Rabbi x says, "He shall. . . ." The result is the appearance of direct speech. In reality, names separate two contradictory apodases to a single protasis (Green, 1979).

Mishnah, then, not only imposes its limited repertoire of forms and formularies throughout, leaving no hint of idiomatic speech (Neusner, 1981). That understates matters. Mishnaic editors deny individuality and personal identity to the rabbis whose names appear across every chapter. Mishnah's rhetoric leaves little room for speech emerging from the individual rabbi's will and intellect. Thus the same words may be put in the mouth of Yohanan b. Nuri as were attributed to Dosa b. Harkinas. Or the same stich might appear anonymously. Gamaliel may be made to parrot the same language, such as, "He is liable," in response to a variety of cases.

Where no room is left for the aspects of personal identity, the category, moral, as normally understood, remains problematic. In Mishnah the denial of individuality extends to speaking; the mishnaic corpus, therefore, does not portray acts of speech. Most of what Mishnah puts in the mouth of rabbis, then, cannot be read as functioning as a model for moral discourse. For neither "moral" nor "discourse" would appear apt categories.

Mishnaic rhetoric in the final analysis devalues rabbinic dialogue and speech. Mishnah favors an artificial, entirely uniform and rather other-worldly language to anything that could be deemed personal, and therefore potentially moral, expression. Mishnah uses a timeless, non-human and utopian mode of communication (see Neusner, 1981). Perhaps its editors thereby bolster the claim for Mishnah's divine origins, while retaining a role for individual human tradents, the rabbis (see Neusner, 1981).

One must seriously consider that much of the discourse in Mishnah's narratives exhibits the forms and formularies in evidence throughout the non-narrative materials. If so, what Mishnah denies to the rabbis of attributed legal sayings, namely, personal identity and speech, the document also withholds from rabbis in narrative contexts. Their individuality too Mishnah eliminates; their putative speech too has none of the qualities of idiomatic identity and of human will. The Aqiva of the narrative speaks in the same Mishnaic rhetoric upon which no real interpersonal communication could be modelled. One cannot say of such narrative discourse that the editor counsels succinct speech of this type, for the rhetoric of Mishnah is too truncated to function as real, effective, interpersonal communication; that precisely is the point of Mishnaic rhetoric.

To a large degree what I maintain about Mishnah's narratives holds as well for Tosefta's. To be sure the editors of Tosefta have played a comparatively minor role in the formulation of pericopae (Neusner, 1977). But the forms or formularies of Toseftan pericopae appear determined in the main by the language of correlative Mishnaic passages (Neusner, 1977). Tosefta, however, preserves as well materials independent of Mishnah. Perhaps here my claims may warrant significant qualification. That remains to be seen, following careful and detailed analysis of the source at hand.

In the final analysis, then, I caution those who would see in earliest rabbinic narratives norms for interpersonal communication in any real sense of the term. These narratives share in the overall linguistic and formal traits of Mishnaic sayings. And for this reason I must judge narrative discourse as part and parcel of Mishnah's rejection of real speech by real people.

TOWARD A SEMIOTIC STUDY OF JEWISH MORAL DISCOURSE: THE CASE OF RESPONSA

Peter J. Haas
Vanderbilt University

ABSTRACT

The characteristic rabbinic format for casting moral discourse is the responsum. In these texts, specific moral or legal issues are addressed and proper actions defined. This essay shows that we can adduce rabbinic morality not only from the content of these discussions but also from the very way in which they are framed. The case at hand concerns a terminally ill woman, in great pain, who is begging her family to pray for her quick death. The author Hayyim Palaggi, concludes that such a prayer is inappropriate but that the family may stop praying for her continued life. This essay examines how this point is argued and articulated. Two aspects of responsa writing in particular are examined. One is the legal character of the language used. This, it is claimed, links the discussion to the Talmud and so ultimately back to Sinai. The other is the use of rabbinic tales as paradigms of virtuous lives.

A translation of the responsum considered here is provided at the end of the essay.

i

All religions attempt to shape the lives of their followers: to prohibit some activities and to encourage others. Although countless attempts have been undertaken to study and compare what kinds of lifestyles these communities define as good, we do not yet have an adequate understanding of what a conception of "the good" is and how such a conception is passed down from generation to generation. Thus we know a good deal about the content of various ethics, but we still know very little about what it means to have an ethic. The purpose of this essay is to investigate what an ethic is by examining how ethical values are transmitted through moral discourse. That is, if we can achieve insight into how moral knowledge is formulated and transmitted, we will have a better idea of what constitutes moral knowledge. This will help us in turn develop a more sophisticated definition of the nature of ethics as a human and cultural creation.

The methodology proposed here make certain assumptions about the nature of ethics and moral discourse. In particular it assumes that moral rules define a system of behavior that is the surface expression of an interlocking grid of deep-seated convictions. Thus moral rules are not simply random adjudications, but are more or less adequate expressions of inarticulated patterns of thought and value. It also assumes that moral discourse is *moral* discourse because it expresses its conclusions in a way that links them to the grid of values and principles which implicitly constitute the hearer's notion of the good or proper life. This means that moral discourse consists not only of what is said, but also of how and in what context it is said. In short, the rhetoric of moral discourse is itself an integral expression of that culture's moral universe. That is why moral discourse itself is a relevant subject for the study of religious ethics.

One purpose of this enterprise is to rethink the way in which comparative religious ethics is done. All to often this has been a matter of collecting rules on one or another theme and setting these next to another list of rules for comparison. While interesting differences or convergences do at times appear, this kind of study is not able to account for these. Most explanation along these lines is little more than a restatement of the data. What is missing is a systematic attempt to get at the culture's deeper mental and emotional structures which bind the diverse rules together into a coherent whole. The claim advanced here is that a comparison of these fundamental systems of convictions offers a much more fruitful activity for understanding how one moral system differs from another and finally for understand what a moral system is at all.

In what follows, I shall examine classical rabbinic moral discourse as found in the responsa literature. The responsa literature is particularly apt for the kind of study proposed here for a number of reasons. It is, to begin with, the most characteristic mode of classical rabbinic moral discourse. Responsa arise in the ninth century as a vehicle for the central Jewish authorities in Babylonia to issue and justify rulings on legal or moral questions addressed to them from distant parts of the Arab empire. In this they resemble the older Roman rescripts and the Moslem *fatwa*. By the Middle Ages, these documents were being produced by the thousands by local rabbinic authorities, dealing with every imaginable question. Insofar as responsa became in effect the standard genre of rabbinic moral writing, I take them to be the appropriate subject for a study of classical rabbinic moral rhetoric. These texts are useful also because they not only state the ruling, but routinely justify it with lengthy argumentation. They thus show us how the rabbis supposed that moral rules are to be explained and warranted to their public. In light of the discussion above, we shall want to study not the content of these rescripts, but rather their rhetoric, the values and logic which give them structure and meaning to their readers. As we shall see, these documents offer rich insight into the grammar of Jewish moral discourse, that is, into those features that make Jewish ethics systematically different from other ethics. Before turning to our analysis, however, I want to establish the methodological parameters within which we shall work.

We begin by noting that there are two ways in which our investigation might proceed. On the one hand, anthropologists of law, such as Leopold Pospisil, attempt to discern how a legal system implicitly defines legal relationships. That is, they want to discover what precisely a legal system means by words or concepts such as ownership, acquisition, liability and so forth. [The aim, we might say, is to discover the content of the law.] On the other hand, philosophers of law have focussed on what we might call the structure of law, that is, how these concepts are brought meaningfully into play. The aim is to discover the rules of the game, that is, how actual legislation and adjudication are to take place. In short, this line of research asks how a society structures and institutionalizes its legal speculation.

The methodology proposed here focusses on these latter issues, the structure of the law. In particular, it asks how rabbinic Judaism organizes and controls the production of legal and moral norms. Our approach, then, is to be distinguished from the field of "Hebrew Law" *(Mishpat Ivri)* which has to do with the content of Jewish legal terms and concepts, and so is a part of the field of anthropology of law. We are concerned rather with the values and convictions which determine how Jewish law is to be produced, justified and adjudicated in the first place. We want to determine what can count as a Jewish law, and why. For this reason we shall draw heavily on the philosophy of law.

Before framing our techniques of analysis, we must have a clear conception of what it is we want to learn. My inspiration in this regard comes from H. L. A. Hart. According to Hart, any system of rules, such as a legal system, can be understood to operate on two levels. On the one hand are what he calls the primary rules, the overt regulations the system imposes. Behind these stands a set of "secondary rules": the procedures and norms according to which the primary rules are legitimately established. These may be written out explicitly, as in the U.S. Constitution, or may be part of a generally accepted understanding of how the creation of rules and the adjudication of disputes ought properly to take place. In either case, these secondary rules reflect the values and principles which define that society's notion of good and evil. In other words, secondary rules spell out, in practical terms, how good is to be distinguished from evil, who is empowered to make that decision, and how that person is to do so and so forth. Any study of a legal system, Hart says, must aim to uncover those hidden "secondary rules" which stand behind and legitimate the group's overt norms of behavior.

For guidance in devising a methodology for getting at these rules, we go back to the pioneering work of John Ladd on Navajo ethics. In his study, Ladd wanted to produce a description of the Navajo system of ethics that would capture the unique logic of that system and not merely transfer it into Western philosophical terms. Whether he succeeded or not is not our concern. What is of interest is the methodology he proposes for carrying out such an analysis. He proposed to base his investigation on the way the Navajo actually talked about their own moral code. That is, he proposed to study the linguistic universe in which their ethics found expression. His insight, which I follow here, is that moral decisions are not episodic, but reflect a deeper system which is organized by, or at least reflected in, language. His methodology, then, was designed to work with actual Navajo discourse and to uncover the rules and presuppositions which give it structure and meaning. Consequently, he focusses on those features of moral speculation which predominate in language: vocabulary, the structure of moral arguments, the warrants that are invoked and so forth. Ladd explains his choice this way:

> [I]t is clear that our primary evidence for determining a person's ideas, whether they be ethical or nonethical, must be that person's statements. Such statements are a *sine qua non* and, as such, the obvious starting point for an investigation of his beliefs. This follows from the philosophical consideration that a belief cannot be defined in terms of readiness to act or some kind of operational efficacy. . . . (p. 15)

In other words, to get at the basic convictions and beliefs held by members of a society about the good life, we must first see how members of that society talk to each other about the good life. This is not only a matter of seeing what people claim they should or should not do. It is, more importantly, a matter of seeing how people explain their decisions and what values and beliefs these explanations assume others already accept as self-evident. It means adducing the precise connotations conjured up by words such as good, evil, warrant, sin, intent, act and the like. It means also describing how these words function in relation to each other in the speakers' and hearers' minds. In short, it means describing the linguistic universe in which a culture's moral discourse takes place.

There are several adjustments we must make in applying Ladd's methodology to medieval Jewish responsa. Ladd fashioned his method on the assumption that he could interview his informants. He could hear their responses and probe for clarification when the logic or vocabulary used was not clear to him. This gives him a mechanism for controlling his interpretation. We do not have this control available when dealing with responsa. All we have at our disposal are essays, the authors of which are long dead and the content of which we can only partially reconstruct. Further, we cannot even read all of these essays. We must choose some small sampling and hope that these adequately represent how Jews in a certain time and place actually discussed moral issues. Thus while I am attracted to Ladd's basic approach, I recognize that it must be modified to be appropriate for our evidence. Let me explain how I propose to make that transition.

I begin by noting that despite the drawbacks of the literature, responsa have a number of features which recommend them for such an analysis. First of all, they are as close as we are likely to get to how their authors might actually discuss moral questions. They take up actual moral dilemmas. That is, they deal with issues of immediate and practical concern, not primarily with academic or philosophical concerns. They are discursive and so reflect the syntax and logic of moral discourse in a way that a code of law, or a philosophical treatise, does not. With such texts we are at least within hailing distance of the kind of moral talk that Ladd could hear. Finally, they are the characteristic format for medieval rabbinic moral writing. That is, they are the commonly accepted way, at least among the intellectual elite, for discussing ethics. Responsa thus match in many ways the characteristics of moral discourse that Ladd found so compelling.

Having selected responsa as a promising corpus of literature, reflective of actual discourse, however, we must still devise a scheme for dealing with them as literature. Because the responsa are highly legal in character, I turn to philosophers of law for aid in constructing an analytic strategy. For this, I rely primarily on Ronald Dworkin. Dworkin claims that any legal argument or decision is an act of judicial discretion. That is, the judge, at least in interesting cases, never mechanistically applies the law to some situation. Rather, he uses his taste and judgment to determine what the law ought to do and then fashions an opinion with its warrants in light of that determination. A correct analysis of any legal brief, on this view, must look behind the surface of the law to the penumbra of values and principles which surround the judge's decision and upon which he draws. These values and principles, Dworkin goes on to say, are part of the cultural baggage the judge brings to his office. It follows that correct analyses of a number of more or less contemporary cases will illuminate the general expectations and values current in a culture at that time. The upshot is that Dworkin forces us to shift our focus away from the surface of the argument used to warrant a decision, and toward the deeper convictions that determine and shape that argument. This description of matters provides us with an analytic scheme.

We carry on the methodological parallel to Ladd's interviews by reading each text and asking ourselves what the basic values and principles behind it must be. That is, we look for the deeper convictions at play in the writer's mind as he reaches and then justifies a certain point of view. To confirm our reading, we of course can not ask for the writer's reaction to our conclusions. Rather we will have to analyze a number of comparable texts to see if our results are replicable over a number of "interviews."

An analysis of the type called for by Dworkin requires that we have some familiarity with how legal arguments are put together and made to function. For understanding the character of argumentative texts, I find Chaim Perelman to be convincing, and, as we shall see, appropriate to the responsa literature. Perelman claims that any legal argument is ultimately a kind of syllogism. At some point in the argument, the judge asserts some good which the law is meant to establish. This functions as a major normative premise. The particular interpretation given to the issue at hand becomes the minor premise. The resulting argumentation simply shows that if one reads the conflict at hand in this way in light of the asserted goal of the law, then one particular adjudication naturally follows. For example, a judge might posit as a major premise that a goal of law is to prevent the taking of innocent human life. This assertion would reflect, in Dworkin's terms, the values of the society in which the legal adjudication occurs. It would appear to be more or less self-evident. The next step is to read the case at hand, say a question of abortion, in light of this premise. An abortion might be described as the taking of an innocent human life. This description of matters, in effect a minor premise, is a matter of judicial discretion. It is not explicitly written into the law (or there would be no case), but is asserted by the judge. This reading will once again reflect broader cultural values. Once matters are presented in this way, Perelman argues, the judge's decision appears to flow logically. Abortion appears self-evidently illegal.

The important point to note here is that according to Perelman both the major premise (the basic good the law seeks) and the minor premise (the character of the issue) are subjective determinations. That is, in each case they are posited by the judge on the basis of what he, and supposedly the consensus of his culture, deem to be self-evidently the case. Perelman's analysis helps us conceive more precisely a strategy for analyzing a responsum and adducing its underlying penumbra of values and principles. We must first identify the basic structure of the responsum's argument, especially noting its major and minor premises. This done, we then reconstruct from the wording and logical use of these premises, the values, principles and assumptions which they instantiate. This, in turn gives us evidence of the broader system of convictions out of which the responsum grows.

APPLYING THE METHOD

My intention in what follows is to test out this methodology by applying it to a particular responsa text. I want to see what insight I can gain into the rabbinic universe of moral discourse by reading their responsa. The text I propose to use is *Hikkeke Lev* 50, written by Hayyim Palaggi (1788–1869) in the early nineteenth century. Hayyim Palaggi was the scion of a well-known rabbinic family in Izmir, Turkey. His father held the office of chief rabbi *(haham bashi)* of Izmir, a position Hayyim took over in 1852. Because of his position and his own reputation as scholar, Palaggi received questions from Jewish communities all over the Near East and North Africa. A first collection of his responsa was published in Salonika in 1840, entitled *Hikkeke Lev* (i.e. "searchings of the heart", cf Judges 5:15). It is from this volume that our responsum is taken. A second volume appeared in 1853. Scholars agree that these two volumes include but a small portion of Palaggi's total writings.

I choose the responsum before us for a number of reasons. First of all its topic is accessible to us. The text does not deal with an obscure point of Jewish law but with a problem of medical ethics that is still with us, namely, the extent to which one must go to save the life of a terminally ill and dying patient. Second, it treats its subject in such a way that non-specialists can follow its argument. It does not presuppose rabbinic familiarity with Jewish law. Finally, it does all of this in reasonable length. Combined with the fact that Palaggi was widely recognized as a competent spokesman of Jewish law make this text ideal for the study proposed here.

We begin our analysis by examining the values and presuppositions that stand behind the responsa *qua* responsa. That is, we begin by asking what we can learn about rabbinic moral discourse from the fact that we have responsa at all. Once the broader features of the literature have been reviewed, we can turn to their particular manifestation our text. I want to focus attention in particular on three major formal aspects that our text shares with all responsa: the character of the writer, the character of the audience, and the program of the text, i.e. what it is meant to communicate.

A responsum, as we said earlier, is a written brief dealing with some aspect of Jewish practice, custom, belief or interpretation. It is composed in answer to specific questions which are addressed to the author and which are deemed of general interest. In the ninth and tenth centuries, the time of our earliest extant responsa, such questions were addressed to the Geonim—the deans of the great Talmudic acadamies then flourishing in Abbasid Babylonia. As heads of these centers, they were held to be the ultimate authority as regards the proper understanding and application of Talmudic law. Their responsa, which survive by the hundreds, are very brief, often consisting only of a precis of the question and a word or phrase to indicate the answer.

By the eleventh century this pattern is changing. From this time forward, questions are more and more likely to be addressed to local rabbinic authorities in North Africa or Europe rather than to the distant Geonim. This shift is a result of a number of factors: the political tensions between North African and European rulers on the one hand and the Abbasid Caliphate on the other, the rise of local rabbinates, the general decline of the Babylonian academies. In all events, we see responsa from this period forward as exercises in local rabbinic authority rather than as official pronouncements of policy issuing from a centralized "bureaucracy."

This shift in venue has important implications for the analysis to follow. The Geonim had authority by virtue of their position in the Jewish world. They headed the recognized centers of Talmudic study. The local rabbis who emerge as authors in the eleventh century and following have no such natural base for claiming authority. They depend on whatever reputation they can build as to the reliability of their work. Their work is known, however, solely through the responsa they author. It follows that now the argumentation of the responsa will become crucial for establishing and projecting rabbinic authority. It is for this reason that I find responsa such convincing sources for discovering the nature of classical rabbinic views on the moral life. Responsa are designed, as it were, to gain public acceptance by providing arguments and warrants that are in accord with what the readership—primarily other rabbis, rabbinic students and educated laypersons—expect. To sum up, classical responsa will always be written by rabbis, i.e. experts in Talmud. This establishes the rabbi as the kind of person who has the authority to make moral decisions. They are written to educated laypeople (or even other rabbis) to deal, generally, with real life situations. Their program is not only to state the ruling, but logically to tie that ruling into the larger structure of Jewish tradition. We shall return to these themes later and see how they are manifest in our particular text.

Let us now turn to the specifics of the text at hand. The question, as I said, deals with a family's obligation toward a dying wife and mother. The question as it comes before Palaggi is of course not framed in medical terms, but as a question of religious ritual. The family wants to know whether or not they may, or even must, pray for the continued life of the dying woman who is suffering greatly in the final stages of a terminal disease. Since the family clearly thinks prayer is efficacious, their request is equivalent, in our terms, to withholding medication or the like. The moral question is whether or not these may ever purposely be denied to a patient. In particular, are we morally justified in withholding them if the patient requests that they be withheld? It is with this issue that Palaggi must wrestle.

The responsum yields data on several levels. To begin with, we have Palaggi's own solution to the dilemma at hand. He declares, as we shall see, that the family may indeed stop praying for the suffering woman's continued life, although they may not pray that she actually die. Strangers, on the other hand, may pray for her quick and painless death. It is in order to adduce and justify this rather delicate balance that the responsum is written.

There are, however, at least two other levels of analysis. The first has to do with how the responsum puts together its argument. This is the level of analysis pointed to by Perelman. In fact, as we shall see, the real work of the responsum is in warranting the decision, not in stating it. What we see in this text, then, is an example of what counts as legal (or moral) argumentation and proof in classical rabbinic Judaism. What we are looking for is not only the answer, but how Palaggi establishes the answer: how he defines the problem, what evidence he marshalls, and how he manipulates the evidence to produce his results. In short, we are looking for the logic and structure of Palaggi's moral discourse.

These results lead to our last level of analysis, the level dealing with the "subconscious" convictions that make the structure and logic of Jewish moral discourse self-evidently true for Palaggi and his readers. It is here that we get to the questions pursued by Ladd and Dworkin. At this point we ask why the moral discourse as we find it in the responsum takes the form that it does. To help us at this stage of inquiry, I propose to draw on some of the methods of structuralism. To anticipate my conclusions, I shall argue that *Ḥikeke Lev* 50 is effective because it shows that what appears as a conflict on the experiential level is resolved within the semantics of the rabbinic universe of discourse. Thus the answer is shown to be already inherent in the world of rabbinism while the power of that world to solve apparent conflicts is reaffirmed. This occurs because the author is able to manipulate linguistic symbols according to accepted rules and patterns. We shall return to this presently.

ii

The function of a responsum, as we noted, is to advance and justify a legal decision when two apparently irreconcilable demands come into conflict. The first step in analyzing a responsum, then, is to note the conflict out of which it grows and which it is meant to bridge. In the case before us, the family is caught between the humanitarian need to end the woman's suffering and the religious-moral obligation to preserve life at all costs. As the case is presented to us, these two obligations are mutually exclusive. That is, family members must either fulfill their obligation to do whatever they can to preserve her life, thereby extending the woman's agony, or they can accept her wishes to stop praying for her life, thereby violating their obligation to maintain human life. The problem is urgent because the woman is suffering daily and begging for death. Being presented with this situation, Palaggi has two tasks before him, as we have seen. He must make some decision as to what they ought actually to do. But he must also demonstrate to them that his decision does not violate any of the basic moral principles of Torah to which they adhere. Let us now see how Palaggi does this.

Our first step in analyzing the responsum is to note the general structure of its argument. We can discern fairly easily three stages in his presentation. The first stage (2:21–4:19) sets forth the basic legal and moral principles which are relevant to this case and with which we shall be working. The large central section of the text (4:20–9:21) examines the particulars of the case at hand in light of these principles. Here Palaggi concludes that the normal restraints against praying for another's death do not apply to the case at hand. The last section of the responsum (9:22–11:23) adduces the practical advice to be given the family. Since the normal restraints do not fully apply here, the family can at least stop praying for her continued life.

Even this brief overview makes it clear that the organization of the responsum corresponds to the logical scheme that Perelman sees in all legal arguments. Part one of the responsum presents what Perelman would call the major premises—the legal and moral principles—with which we shall be working. Part two presents the minor premises, that is, the relevant descriptions of the case at hand. It also includes part of Perelman's third stage, the drawing of syllogistic conclusions. In this case the results, as we said, are negative. The major premises presented at the outset do not apply. Part three draws the obvious conclusion which follows upon applying the minor premises to the major ones. Since the major premises do not apply, we are allowed to do what they prohibit. Our analysis so far shows that each of the text's major segments employs its own logic and makes its own fundamental moral decisions. It will be necessary, then, to examine each individually.

We begin by looking at how Palaggi defines the whole question. This will allow us to identify the specific considerations and moral rules that will be relevant. As we noted, there are two principles that come into conflict here: relieving agony and preserving life. In his responsum, Palaggi hardly discusses the first topic at all. He simply assumes the legal and moral imperative to relieve pain. He takes it to be self-evident. He finds it necessary to discuss only the second principle. How far must one go in preserving life, especially if one is dealing with a dying patient in terrible agony? The responsum, it turns out, is in fact an essay concerned with this latter point, namely, on the moral obligation to continue life beyond a certain point. By simply framing the question in this way, Palaggi has predetermined at least the general character of his decision. He is looking for a loophole in the imperative to continue preserving life, not in the imperative to stop pain.

His examination into the nature of the imperative to preserve life runs roughly as follows. He notes, first of all, that it is a general principle in Jewish law that one may not hope that other people come to harm, and especially one may not hope that others die (2:21–3:7). This principle applies with special force as regards one's spouse (3:7–4:19). So far, then, it appears that there is a clear prohibition against the family's doing anything to hasten the death of the sick woman. To do so would violate not only the general command to protect the lives of fellow human beings, but runs against the specific obligation towards one's spouse. This will be the major premise of the discussion to follow.

The second stage of the responsum examines the specifics of the case at hand in light of the major premise posited above. In the following paragraphs, Palaggi will argue that the case at hand does not fall under the rule of the major premise. This is so, he argues, for several reasons. First of all, we need to understand the rationale behind the prohibition wishing harm or death to one's spouse. The prohibition assumes, says Palaggi, that the husband would harbor such a wish for his own benefit—he might wish to marry his wife's sister, for example. (see for example 5:15–17; 6:10–15, 6:24–28). This clearly is not the case here. As we have seen, his wish grows out of concern for the welfare of his wife. Further, the prohibition assumes that the wish is formed without the spouse's knowledge and consent (see 7:1ff). This is also clearly not the case here. The wife is in fact begging the family to pray for her death. The results of our analysis of the case, then, shows that it is in fact not covered by the general rule laid down in part one. We can conclude at this point that there is no reason for preventing the family from praying for the victim's quick death.

There is another consideration, however, which Palaggi wishes to take into account before rendering a final decision. What Palaggi has shown so far is that the normal prohibitions against praying for another's death do not apply to the case before us. But there may be other reasons for prohibiting such prayers. In particular, there is concern that allowing prayers for death in some cases might lead to a general softening of the prohibition, and thus to sinful prayers, in the future. For this reason Palaggi counsels caution. Prayers for the woman's quick death might be allowable in principle, but practical considerations stand in the way.

Let us pause briefly to sum up our results so far. First of all, Palaggi wants to emphasize that the prohibition against wishing harm to others is real and deserves serious consideration. But he also finds it perfectly permissible to limit this prohibition by considering intent. For

Palaggi, and he assumes also for his readers, the law is not only what is done but what is intended. Third, public appearance is regarded as a legitimate moral concern which can limit what might otherwise be permitted. We see a number of assumptions about the nature of ethics and moral speculation being rather routinely drawn into the discussion.

Let us now turn to the third section of Palaggi's answer, namely, his own conclusions as to what the family and others can do. He rules that the family may grant her entreaties and withhold prayers that postpone her death. This follows from the first section of the responsum. We cannot, however, allow the family to pray explicitly for her death. This is because of the practical considerations discussed near the end of part two. In other words, while the family is excused from praying that she live, they may not pray explicitly that she die. Such prayers for death are prohibited for practical reasons. Palaggi is afraid that if they were allowed to pray for their relative's death, this would become a precedent for other families with less lofty motives. To avoid all ambiguity, he rules that no family member may ever explicitly pray for the death of another family member. Strangers are another matter, however. We can allow friends or strangers to do what is unseemly for a family member to do. The former may openly pray for the victim's quick release from suffering.

LOOKING BEYOND THE TEXT

We have seen the particular assumptions about the logic of the good life that Palaggi himself makes. There is however a wider range of principles and convictions of the moral life within which Palaggi's decisions occur. The responsum-form itself establishes certain parameters which shape the nature of Jewish moral discourse, parameters which Palaggi takes for granted. It is to these contours, set by the responsum-form, that we now turn.

By establishing its discourse in this way, the responsum allows Palaggi to accomplish several things. He is able, first of all to leave intact the moral values which generated the problem to begin with. The family's feeling of pity is validated. The principle of not invoking death on others is likewise reaffirmed. Yet a workable compromise between the two is adduced. This reconciliation is not presented, however, as the private opinion of Hayyim Palaggi. Rather it is presented as an entailment of the logic of the law. That is, through its stylized language and patterns of argumentation, the responsum presents Palaggi's compromise as in complete continuity with the received legal tradition. This is of vital importance because at one and the same time, it validates the received tradition, offers essentially new legislation, and affirms the power and integrity of the entire rabbinic system of moral speculation. I want at this point to examine some of the elements of discourse which enable the responsum to do this. That is, I want to understand how it is that a responsum can allow the family to stop praying for the woman's death with a clear conscience, something they could not do before.

iii

The responsum–form structures moral discourse in a number of ways. Because of limited space it will be impossible to deal with all of them. I do however wish to reflect on two aspects of this responsum's moral discourse which appear to be of special importance. The first is the use it makes of the story of Rabbi's death (7:5-17). The second is the legal nature of its language and discussion. I claim that both of these elements represent convictions about moral discourse that Palaggi's Jewish readers were assumed to hold. That is, the discussion which makes up the responsum draws on notions about the nature of the world such that its conclusions appear to be self-evidently true. We turn first to the story of Rabbi's death.

This story seems particularly appropriate to the problem at hand. Rabbi is in the process of dying. He is prevented from doing so by his students, who continue to pray for his life. A loyal member of his household (in this case, a maidservant), moved by his agony, interrupts these prayers and so allows Rabbi to die. The fact that this incident is relayed without negative comment indicates to Palaggi that the maidservant's actions are deemed to be appropriate. The point of the story, in his view, is that it is permissible to pray that a suffering person die so as to find rest from agony.

Having rehearsed the story, we must now ask how it functions as a morally persuasive argument for Palaggi's nineteenth century readers. The answer I believe lies in the symbolic value that Talmud has for the family. For classical Judaism, the Talmud is more than a collection of arcane laws and unusual stories. It is a sacred text which through its very logic and structure reveals the logic of the universe. What happens in Talmud, then, is never trivial or of mere antiquarian interest. It is, by definition, of cosmic significance. The story of Rabbi's death then, contains in it a cosmic truth. If its story is your story, then its resolutions are, by the nature of things, your resolution. Put in these terms, the story here is, in History of Religion terms, a myth. That is, it is a description or model or paradigm for a general truth. By bringing this story into relation with the issue at hand, Palaggi establishes a powerful pattern for organizing moral discussion. We see the logic of the issue at hand in terms of the structure of canonical stories. The dying rabbi is our woman, the loyal students are the members of her family, the maidservant is the person behind the question. The relationships these people bear to each other in the story indicate the relationships that ought to obtain in real life.

Just as this story helps organize the facts in our case, the legal language of the texts sets the rules by which any ethical dilemma can be discussed. Legal language is of course characteristic of responsa. For this reason it is often taken for granted. My claim, however, is that this mode of discourse is so widely adopted because it reflects very basic assumptions about the character of revelation, ethics, and so the kind of discourse appropriate to making moral decisions. I therefore wish to examine this language in some detail.

A given fact for rabbinic Judaism is that when God spoke to Moses at Sinai, he uttered the Ten Commandments, that is, God spoke in the language of law. For rabbinic Judaism this does not mean that God simply chose to talk that way that morning. Rather God's language at Sinai reflects a fundamental truth. Torah, that is revelation, is to be articulated and evaluated in the language of law. Or, to state matters another way, the fact that God spoke through law is itself an indication of an even higher reality, namely, the structure of Creation itself. Legal reasoning recapitulates the logic of the cosmos. Thus when God creates the world, he does so through the utterance of regulations. When he creates the holy people of Israel at Sinai, God does so also through the utterance of regulations. It follows that humans following God's pattern of speech, are to structure their own society on the basis of legal discourse.

This reasoning became especially important to the rabbis of the first centuries of the Common Era. They witnessed the destruction of God's holy Temple in Jerusalem and saw what they took to be the dissolution of the Holy people Israel. Creation, in their view, was reverting to the primordial chaos. It was of cosmic importance to them to reverse this process. This conviction was that this could be done only by carrying forward actively and consciously the work of Torah. The people must be reconstituted and the structures of creation reenforced. The model for so doing is Sinai, and the means, clearly, is law. Rabbinic legal activity, then, is understood to be a continuation of that seminal act at Sinai. Given these basic assumptions, the legal nature of responsa becomes religiously powerful. The issuance of a responsum is a kind of giving of the law at Sinai. Not that it is infallible and open to no question. It is still a human endeavor. But insofar as it is an effort to bring into human terms the principles which stand behind Torah and to do so in the semantics of Torah, it has a Sinaitic character.

This discussion of language throws light also on the use of the story discussed earlier. Although the story of Rabbi's death is not Scriptural, it nonetheless protrays the logic of Scripture. Sinai reveals to us models of the good life as well as a language for analyzing and applying those stories to our lives. It provides basic paradigms for structuring our relationships. A responsum provides a forum in which both paradigms—story and discourse—are brought into play so as to include a particular situation within the bonds of Torah. Symbolically, then, a responsum refers us back to Sinai and its role in the founding of the people. It is through symbolic appeal to this myth that the reader is made to feel an obligation to do as the responsum says.

This characterization allows us to make broader claims about responsa as exempla of religious rituals. The responsum, we have said, draws upon the symbols of the Sinaitic revelation and uses them in historical time. Further, we said that it is this ritualistic use of symbol that allows responsa to induce certain moods and motivations in the reader. Clifford Geertz describes this power of religious ritual in his essay "Religion as a Cultural System:"

> As we are to deal with meaning, let us begin with paradigm; *viz.*, that sacred symbols function to synthesize a people's ethos—the tone, character and quality of their life, its moral and aesthetic style and mood—and their world-view—the picture they have of the way things in sheer actuality are, their most comprehensive ideas of order. In religious belief and practice a group's ethos is rendered intellectually reasonable by being shown to represent a way of life ideally adapted to the actual state of affairs the world-view describes, while the world-view is rendered emotionally convincing by being presented as an image of an actual state of affairs peculiarly well arranged to accomodate such a way of life. This confrontation and mutual confirmation has two fundamental effects. On the one hand, it objectivizes moral and aesthetic preferences by depicting them as the imposed conditions of life implicit in a world with a particular structure, as mere common sense given the unalterable shape of reality. On the other, it supports the received beliefs about the world's body by invoking deeply felt moral and aesthetic sentiments as experiential evidence for their truth. Religious symbols formulate a basic congruence between a particular style of life and a specific (if, most often, implicit) metaphysic, and in so doing sustain each with the borrowed authority of the other (Lessa Vogt, p. 167).

A responsum, in short, is a kind of oracle. It motivates me to do as it says because it speaks in the way I know revelation to occur. At the same time it reaffirms my basic religious convictions that the Sinaitic revelation is able appropriately to organize and render meaningful all of my day-to-day activities. There are no conflicts in life that Sinai cannot comprehend.

The story of Rabbi's death and the juridical language of responsa both point, then, to the same transcendent reality. The particular lives of people down here are to be shaped according to the logic which is characteristic of the heavens above. This cosmic structure is made known to people in three ways. It is first of all revealed in the explicit words of Scripture. It is demonstrated, second, in the deeds and actions of the great masters of Torah. Finally, it is developed and articulated through proper legal thinking. Our task is to adduce through these methods the behavior appropriate for dealing with the problems we face in our everyday lives.

iv

We conclude by considering what our investigation into responsa tells us about moral discourse in general. What is required for an imperative to be considered moral, and so binding in a way different from say practical advice or etiquette? The answer seems to lie in the nature of the symbols and values being invoked. Practical advice is meant to produce concrete results. Failure to follow that advice, or failure of the advice to work, does not threaten the stability of the whole culture. The same is true of etiquette. But this is not the case for ethics. The rejection of a society's morals entails the rejection of basic values in that culture.

Responsa shed important light on the relationship between foundational values of a culture and that culture's moral discourse. Consider again the case that comes before Palaggi. We have here a moral dilemma precisely because two foundational values in classical Jewish culture come into conflict. It is at least possible to conceive of a society in which the case before Palaggi would not present moral problems, either because the death of terminally ill people is held to be a promotable good or because suffering in death is understood to be of positive value. The problem is a moral problem for Palaggi (and the family) at all, then, because of the values put forward by their society. The crux of Palaggi's problem is that he must adjudicate between the foundational values without denying either one. He must affirm the validity of the whole system even while dealing with its contradictions. His way of doing this, in the responsa, is through legal argumentation. This mode allows him to take both values seriously and yet, through logical analysis or precedent, create room for an adjudication. It allows him to do this, most importantly, in a way already sanctioned by the system. The result is that everyone wins. The basic values that come into conflict are both upheld. A practical solution to a new problem is legitimately generated. And the process by which this magic is effected is once again shown to be effective—it has allowed us to maneuver through the shoals without accident. In short, the integrity of medieval Jewish legal/moral discourse is maintained. Our foundational values are not only left intact, but are proved and reaffirmed.

The conclusions of a responsum are morally binding, then, in at least one sense, because to ignore the conclusion is to reject the explicit entailments of foundational values, principles, and convictions of that culture. I can, of course, reject his argument and propose another in my own responsum. In this way I still maintain the integrity of the system, focussing my rejection on how the system was used. But if I reject the responsum mode in general, then I am rejecting the system as such. The entire social framework which the system maintains is thrown into doubt. I am bound by the values of the culture, then, to conform to the arguments and adjudications of its responsa, for the alternative is the loss of the culture's values entirely.

Considered in this way, we can describe the writing of responsa as a religious ritual. It is, first of all, a symbolic act which establishes a certain relationship between petitioner, rabbi, and the tradition. That is, responsa act out and reaffirm the flow of power within the community. In addition, by participating in the ritual—asking a question, writing an answer, conforming to its judgment—each party reaffirms his or her own membership in the society. Further, the all-encompassing knowledge of the sacred books and traditions is reaffirmed. A seemingly insolvable dilemma is shown to have a clear resolution in terms of the logic of the sacred. Finally, this act is a ritual insofar as it is resorted to time and again in substantially the same form as crises arise in the lives of people.

We stated at the beginning of this paper that any religion presupposes some system of good and evil which it wishes to legislate. Our goal was to discover the logic and structure of that system. We claimed that this was not to be found simply by restating the content of Jewish law, but rather by analyzing the universe of discourse within which Judaism articulates and justifies its rules. We then proposed to use semiotics as a starting point for devising such a strategy and then to see what results it would yield when applied to a responsum.

The results of our exercise are encouraging. We have in fact been able to adduce data about Jewish moral thinking by analyzing how responsa texts, as examples of moral discourse, are structured. The results of this study are hardly sufficient in themselves, however. We have dealt briefly with only one responsum. Not only could we do more with this one text, but we need to check the method and corroborate our results with similar studies on other texts. In essence then, this essay proposes a program for further study and research. Only through a sustained and systematic study of other responsa, and other types of responsa, can we hope to make a solid advance in the study and understanding of Jewish moral discourse.

TRANSLATION OF THE TEXT

QUESTION: A god-fearing scholar has a pious wife. Because of our many sins this woman has been afflicted with a long-term disease. For more than 20 years she has been crushed and burdened with pain. Her arms and legs have shrivelled up, forcing her to be confined to a corner of her house. This woman suffers greatly from these afflictions. Her husband, however, accepts the suffering of his wife with patience, never troubling her even for a moment. On the contrary, he shows her special affection and love so that she may have no worry on this account.

Because of her unbearable pain, the aforementioned woman has already prayed that God take her. She prefers death to life because in death she will find rest from her pain. Her husband and children, however, may God bless them, comfort her and continually bring her physicians and medicines in the hope that a remission might occur. They have even hired a maid to wait on her so that she should have no worries. Now, as if the continual pain and bitter suffering she has had up to now were not enough, her condition has worsened, bringing with it terrible agony, such as accompany dreadful diseases, leaving her totally stricken and invalid. Even the physicians have given up hope, especially since the disease has affected her internal organs, an event which occurs twenty days before death, as written in Tractate *Semahot* III:11: "For this is the death of the righteous as opposed to the other kinds of plagues, wounds, afflictions and diseases."[1] Recently she began to ask others as well to pray for her death. She especially pleads with her husband and children to intercede on her behalf. But her husband and children, though they are worn out with her suffering, do not listen to her because of their love and affection, she being a righteous and pious woman. On the contrary, they seek scholars who would teach on her behalf so as to bring healing and they increase their giving of charity and paying redemption and atonement money and buying oil for the lamps—all in order to obtain healing for her.

Let our master in righteousness now instruct us as to whether or not there are any grounds for prohibiting prayers that she find rest in death. If there is no prohibition—what if her husband and sons are so concerned with her life that they do not want to see her die? May they pray that she not die, ignoring her own wishes; or, since according to the physicians there is no way she will live and there is no longer hope that she will recover naturally, would this be against her well-being (such that they must pray for her death)?

May the master instruct us and may his portion in heaven be doubled.

ANSWER: First of all, it is clearly forbidden in all cases to pray that another person die. This is so even if one is praying only that some misfortune befall an enemy. Torah commands, for example, that if you see the mule of one who hates you collapse under its burden and you refuse to help, you will be abandoned just as you abandoned the animal (Deut.

22:4). Torah is concerned here that you not cause the animal's owner any material loss. How much the more is Torah concerned that you not cause your enemy to lose his life. Thank God no Jew is suspected of doing this!

There is another prohibition involved, namely, that this kind of curse, in fact any curse on one's fellow, is forbidden. This is so even if done without explicitly naming the intended victim. In fact, if one pronounces a curse on another by name, the curser is flogged, as it is written in (Babylonian Talmud) Temurah 4b. See also Mishneh Torah "Sanhedrin" 27:1 and the Tur Shulchan Aruch and the Shulchan Aruch Hoshen Mishpat 27:1.[2]

We turn now specifically to wishing harm to one's spouse. Our masters, may their memories be a blessing, say in BT Qiddushin 83a, "It is forbidden for one to marry a woman before he sees her lest when he sees her he find something detestable in her and she be disgraced by him—for the Merciful One said, 'You should love your neighbor as yourself.'" This verse, a central rule in the Torah, applies also to one's husband or wife. (Its point is that you should not get yourself in a position in which you might wish harm to your spouse). We learn this same thing from BT Yebamot 37b, "One should not marry a woman with the intention of divorcing her, for it says (in Proverbs 3:29), 'Do not plot evil against your fellow who lives trustingly with you (i.e. your spouse).'" See also the writings of the legal scholars, the Tur and the Shulchan Aruch Even HaEzer top of #119. It is also stated in Avot de Rabbi Nathan (hereafter ARN), chapter 26, "Rabbi Aqiba says, 'Anyone who marries a woman who is not suitable for him transgresses five negative commands: 1) 'Do not take vengeance (Lev. 19:18)', 2) 'Do not bear a grudge (ibid.), 3) 'Do not hate your neighbor in your heart (Lev. 19:17)', 4) 'Love your neighbor as yourself (ibid.)', 5) 'That your brother may live with you (Lev. 25:36).' Further, insofar as he hates her and wishes she would die, he refrains from the command "Be fruitful and multiply."'"

(All the above speak about wishing harm to one's spouse. But the law also speaks specifically about wishing for the spouse's death.) Our masters report in the beginning of Chapter 3 of ARN, for example, "He used to say, 'As for one who wishes his wife to die that he may marry her sister, or anyone who wishes his brother to die that he may marry his wife, his end will be that they (i.e. the intended victims) will bury him during their lifetimes. As regards such a person, Scripture says (Ecclesiates 10:8), 'The one who digs the pit will fall into it; and a serpent will bite the one who breaks through the wall.'" This is to say that if one hopes his wife will die so that he might marry another woman, heaven will arrange for the opposite to occur.

(Can a mere thought be the concern of the law, however?) R. Hayyim Yosef David Azulai writes in *Kise Ra. hamim*, "If one merely has an evil thought, the Holy One, Blessed be He, does not consider it to be an evil deed, and so does not punish that person on its account."[3] This means simply this: that a thought, being insubstantial, that is, without any overt expression, material effect or outward appearance (is not subject to legal punishment). However, on the other hand, BT Sota 9a (bottom) says, "Whoever looks greedily upon what is not his—that which he wants will not be given to him and that which he has will be taken away." (Here Talmud implies that in fact the mere thought is subject to divine punishment.)

Now, in my humble opinion, (the cases assumed by the above rulings) are different from the case before us. All of the aforementioned rulings are based on a particular prohibition from the tradition. The rabbis take the command "Do not devise evil against your fellow (Proverbs 3:29)" to apply to one thinking about divorcing his wife; all the more so to one hoping that she will die. There is also the positive command, "Love your neighbor as yourself" which our rabbis, may their memories be a blessing, apply especially to one's wife. Besides these there is the prohibition of "not hating your brother in your heart (Leviticus 19:17)." This applies not only to brothers, for it is clear that one must love one's wife also and show affection for her—as written in BT Yebamot 72b (bottom), "One who loves his wife as himself . . . (is blessed)." See also what our master and teacher Meir b. Baruch of Rothenburg wrote in his collected responsa 81:30, "As for one who beats his wife, I have learned that we deal with him more harshly than with one who beats his neighbor. For he is not obligated to honor the neighbor, but he is obligated to honor his wife."[4] There is also the prohibition against casting the evil eye on his wife, especially so as to cause her to die. There is also the prohibition recorded in BT Baba Mezia 107a and in Baba Bathra 2b: "It is forbidden for one to cast the evil eye on his neighbors field when it is full of standing grain."

There is an additional danger as well when he fantasizes that his wife dies so that he can marry her sister, or that his fellow dies so that he can marry his wife. In so doing he may have sinful thoughts for he may think about her (i.e. the one he wants to marry) and this thought will bear evil fruit when he has sex, for his children will be surrogate children.[5] Or he might suffer a nocturnal emission. This prohibition comes from BT Nedarim 20a. The legal authorities address this issue, as does AT and SHA in Orah Hayyim 260.

I am inclined to say that what the rabbis, may their memories be a blessing, had in mind when they said, "One who fantasizes that his wife die so that he might marry her sister . . ." was not meant to apply only to her sister.[6] For the law is the same even for one who fantasizes that his wife die so that he might marry any other woman. They take up this case of the sister only because in the time of the Talmud the Ban of Rabbenu Gershom was not in effect, nor was the prohibition of the wedding vow, both of which prohibit one from marrying another woman while married to the first wife.[7] A man could marry another woman, in addition to his first wife, without his first wife having to die. Therefore they cite the case of the wife's sister because he is in all events prohibited from marrying this woman during his wife's lifetime. That is, he must wait for his wife to die before he can marry one of her sisters. Nowadays it is all the same, since he may not have more than one wife, both because of Rabbenu Gershom's Ban and because of the prohibition in the wedding vows. Thus any evil thought that he has that his wife might die so that he can marry another is prohibited. See *Toldot Adam* #4.[8] They also said in Tractate *Derekh Erets Rabbah* 11:13, "Ben Azzai says, "One who hates his wife is a murderer, as it is said, 'He will falsely accuse her and will finally hire witnesses against her and bring her to the execution place'". They also say (*ibid*. 2:12), "One who lives in an obscene manner with his wife or one who tells false tales about her in the neighborhood in order to divorce her, about such a one Scripture says, 'I the Lord investigate the heart and examine the innermost parts (Jeremiah 17:10).'"[9] It turns out that from all that has been said it is forbidden to wish that one's wife die because of hatred. This being so, we deduce (further) that it is absolutely forbidden to pray that anyone die, especially as regards a wife, who is like one's own self.

However, all this appears to apply only if the wish comes from hatred and without the wife's knowledge and consent. But when, to the contrary, she acquiesces to this wish because she no longer can bear the suffering of the body, then we can say that such a wish is permitted. I say this with BT Ketubot 104a in mind:

> On the day that Rabbi died, the sages declared a public fast and they prayed saying, "If anyone says, 'Let Rabbi die'—let that one be run through with a sword." The maidservant of Rabbi went up on the roof and said, 'The angels seek Rabbi and the creatures seek Rabbi. Let it be Thy will that the angels give way to the creatures.' When she reflected on how often Rabbi had entered the privy and taken off his teffilin and put them on and how he was now suffering (she had a change of heart). She prayed, 'Let the angels have way over the creatures.' But the Rabbis did not stop praying (and so Rabbi still did not die). She finally took a jug and threw it among (the praying disciples) from the roof. They stopped praying and Rabbi (immediately) died.[10]

It is clear from this passage that the maidservant of Rabbi, when she saw how he was suffering, prayed for his death. Furthermore, we find in BT Moed Katan 17a and also in some of the pertinent commentaries in Rosh, Tur Shulchan Aruch and Shulchan Aruch Hoshen Mishpat 40:34, that the ancient authorities adduced legal rulings from what Rabbi's maidservant did because she was his servant (and so would surely conduct herself as he instructed her) and also because they deemed her to be a scholar in her own right, being filled with wisdom and the fear of heaven. This being so, we may adduce from this story the following: that it is permitted to pray that the sick person who is suffering greatly might die and so find rest. Were this not so, the Talmud would not have cited this story. Or, had the Talmud meant only to report the event (but with the understanding) that the maidservant acted wrongly, it should have said so explicitly.

Now you might want to argue that, on the contrary, the fact that the masters prayed for Rabbi's life without regard for his suffering ought to be the legal precedent. In response, I would argue that they at first did not pay any attention to his sufferings, while his maidservant did. Later, when they realized how much he was suffering, they in fact did stop praying. Further, it is clear that the rabbis did not disagree with what Rabbi's maidservant did, for had they disagreed they would have rebuked her straightaway, especially since they had just decreed that anyone who said, 'Let Rabbi die' was to be run through with a sword. Surely this should include one who prayed that he should die. Further, had her act been wrong, you would think that the Talmud would not remain silent but would protest that what she did was improper. But since the Talmud does remain silent and since the rabbis appear in fact to agree with the maidservant's actions, the inevitable conclusion is that in the case of the afflicted woman who is ill and suffering much pain and who is begging others to pray that she die, it is certainly entirely permitted to do so. This is now clear.

I also saw in the writings of Rabbenu Nissim to Nedarim 40a: "that we do not need to pray for him at all neither that he live nor that he die."[11] It seems to me that this means that at times one may pray that a sick person die, for instance when the sick person is suffering greatly from his disease and cannot go on living much longer anyway, as we have read in BT Ketubot 104a that when Rabbi's maidservant considered how he entered the privy regularly and always took of his phylacteries and was now suffering, said, 'May it be Thy will that the angels have way over the creatures," that is, that Rabbi be allowed to die.' Thus it is that the prayers of one who visits the sick are efficacious (whether they be for life or for death)." . . .

After several days I came across *Gur Aryeh Judah* by his Excellency Our Master and Teacher Aryeh Judah Leib Teomim and saw that he wrote in *Hiddushe Yore Dea* 260:52, "As regards a sick person for whom they have given up hope and who is suffering greatly—is it permitted to pray that he die?"[12] I looked up the place but I could find no clue as to his answer because the relevant part of the book was missing. In fact, I found that on page 55c at the conclusion of #50—where we should find #51 and #52, in the middle of the column—he begins immediately with #53. The other two paragraphs, namely #51 and #52 are missing from the printing plate. Thus I have no idea what he had written in #52 on this matter—whether I agree with his opinion that it should be permitted to pray for the patient's death, or whether I disagree because he prohibits such a prayer.

It appears in my humblest of opinions that because of all this it makes sense to do as (follows): if she is suffering very much from her many bitter afflictions, and if the physicians all say that there is no hope that she will live and they have given up in despair, then as regards even her husband and children and relatives, if they do not want to pray that she live, let them not pray explicitly that she die, either. Rather, let them sit and do nothing. For if they pray that she die, there is the chance that, heaven forbid, one out of a thousand will see this and come to the unlikely conclusion that he is praying for her death so that he might be free from her and from her demands. That is, someone might assume that he has an interest in her death. This is especially so as regards the husband, for there is always room for the suspicion, heaven forbid, that he desires her death for his own benefit, even if he is pious and a proper scholar. For Scripture says, "I am the Lord who searches the heart and investigates the innermost parts." (That is, only God can know what one really is thinking.) This is referred to several times in ARN.

In all events, the best, in God's eyes, is to make no prayer or petition that she die, even if by refusing to pray for her death he does not show proper respect or compassion for her or the family. He should refrain from praying that she die even if he has her best interests in mind. Now there is something to be said for this view. One surely can make a distinction between what Rabbi's maidservant did in openly praying for his death and what we today may do. If the Talmudic masters could say (in BT Shabbat 112b), "If the earlier sages were sons of men, we are like asses, and not even like the ass of R. Pinhas b. Yair (which was exceptionally pious—Cf BT Hullin 7ab),[13] but like ordinary asses," then surely one can say, "We are not like Rabbi's maidservant and so can not do what she could do."

Now to pray that she live is hard because of the pain she must suffer and the bitter agonies she must endure. If you reflect on the matter you will see that it is not always preferable that she continue to live. On the other hand, as we noted, it is really not proper for them openly to pray that she die, either. However, as for others, who are strangers and not under any of the aforementioned suspicions—if they pray that she die so that her soul might find rest, they may do so. All is according to what is written, "God searches the heart and the innermost parts, the Lord is righteous." Our rabbis, may their memories be a blessing, have said that all that is in the heart is to God as if it were spoken. Therefore fear the Lord.

Now all this applies when the sick person is not actually in the throes of death. However, if that person is in the throes of death, there is no way that one may pray (for continued life). It is written in *The Book of the Pious* #234 that one ought not cry out at the time when the soul leaves the body.¹⁴ The reason for not doing so is that the soul not be induced to return to the body and cause the patient more suffering. Why did Ecclesiastes say there is a time to die? Because when a person dies—when the soul is leaving the body—they ought not cry out loud that the soul return, because the patient cannot live but a few more days anyway and during those days would suffer nothing but agonies. (This line of reasoning is not negated by the fact that Ecclesiastes) also says "a time to live" because human beings have no control over the time of death. We may conclude, then, that according to *The Book of the Pious*, one is not to pray for a person who is in the throes of death. See also what Isserles writes in his gloss to Shulchan Aruch Yore Dea #339.

That is what, in my humble opinion, I must write, although in haste because the strength of the sufferer is weak. May Almighty God say "enough" to our troubles and save us from error and show us wonders from the Torah. May this be God's will. Amen.

NOTES

[1] This is the classical rabbinic text dealing with matters of death and mourning. It is appended to the BT, although it is generally assumed by modern scholars to have been written after the Talmud. The euphemistic title *Sema . hot* ("rejoicings") replaced its original name *Evel Rabbati* ("Major Tractate on Mourning") in the Middle Ages. The cited passage reads as follows: "Rabbi Judah said:, 'The early Hasidim used to be afflicted with intestinal illness for about 10 to 20 days before their deaths, so that they might be wholly purged and arrive pure in the hereafter . . ." The translation is from D. Zlotnick, *The Tractate "Mourning"* (Yale Judaica Series, ed. Leon Nemoy, New Haven: Yale U. Press, 1966), p.39.

[2] "One who curses any Jew, by name or designation, or any of the names which non-Jews refer to the Holy One—if this one was warned in front of witnesses, he is given one lash of the whip for transgressing Scripture's prohibition, 'Do not curse the deaf.' If this one (i.e. the victim) is a judge, (the one who cursed him) is given a second lash because he transgressed the command, 'Do not curse God (the judge being taken as a symbol of God's presence)' . . .

[3] Hayyim Yosef David Azulai was connected with a Talmudic academy in Hebron in the late nineteenth century and traveled widely on its behalf. *Kise Ra . hamim*, a commentary on ARN was published in Leghorn, Italy in 1803, a short time before his death.

[4] Meir ben Baruch was one of the leaders of the Jewish intellectual revival in central Europe in the thirteenth century.

[5] This superstition holds that if the husband is thinking of another woman while having sex with his wife, the resulting conceptus will be, in some sense, the offspring of the second woman.

[6] According to Jewish law a man may not be married to a woman and her sister at the same time. If he wants to marry the sister, he must first dissolve the current marriage.

[7] Gersom ben Judah was one of the first great Talmudic scholars in Europe. He flourished in the early eleventh century. The ban referred to here prohibits bigamy, a practice technically allowed under Jewish law. The wedding vow has the husband pledge not to take on a second wife while the marriage is in effect.

[8] This is the name of the second volume of responsa written by Solomon ben Adret. Adret, who was a widely-recognized authority, lived in Barcelona, Spain all of his life (1235–1310).

[9] *Derekh Erets Rabbah* ("The Great Tractate on Good Conduct") along with a smaller text on the same theme make up a minor tractate in the Babylonian Talmud. Although parts of the tractate may go back to Talmudic times, most scholars agree that it is a later work. The tracate consists mostly of ethical rules and aphorisms.

[10] According to BT Baba Metzia 85a, Rabbi suffered for thirteen years from *"smyrt'"* and *"sprn'"* (translated by I. Epstein as kidney stone and scurvy. See "Baba Mezia" in *The Babylonian Talmud* (London: Soncino, 1935), p. 486. Cf Marcus Jastrow, *A Dictionary of the Targumim, the Talmud Babli, etc* II:1288). The story here assumes that Rabbi had to make frequent, and painful, trips to the privy. Despite his disability, he always was careful to remove his prayer accoutrements so as to accord them due honor.

[11] Nissim ben Reuben Gerondi, A Spanish talmudist of the fourteenth century.

[12] A leading Galician rabbi. He served as rabbi of Brody, now in the Soviet Union, until his death in 1831.

[13] According to the Talmudic story, the donkey in question refused to eat fodder put before it until tithes had been properly removed.

[14] *The Book of the Pious* is a moral text reflecting the religious beliefs of a pietistic Jewish sect that flourished in Germany during the twelfth and thirteenth centuries.

RESPONSE TO PETER HAAS SEMIOTICS AND JEWISH ETHICS

Daniel Patte
Vanderbilt University

Peter Haas is to be commended for his pioneering essay which proposes a program for studying Jewish ethics "that will reveal the systematic logic at work behind a moral system, the processes of thought that bring its particular rules, definitions, and decisions together to form a meaningful and coherent whole." The very goal of this project distinguishes it from the field of "Hebrew Law" *(Mishpat Ivri)*; the focus is no longer on the content of Jewish law, but on how it is to be "produced, justified and adjudicated." Consequently, the vast corpus of Jewish legal material needs to be viewed from the "outside" rather than from the "inside." Rather than staying in the boundaries of the Jewish legal discourse so as to "understand it in its own terms," Haas strives to elucidate what these "terms" are which govern it, and for this purpose he needs to stand outside of it by considering the Jewish legal discourse from the perspective of general theories concerning legal discourses and ethics (or, more specifically, religious ethics). Thus, Haas calls upon works on philosophy of law by H. L. A. Hart, Ronald Dworkin, and Chaim Perelman, on Navajo ethics by John Ladd, and on religious ritual and ethics by Clifford Geertz.

This is a pioneering essay in a twofold sense. First, although such theories have already informed in various ways studies of the Jewish legal corpus, Haas proposes to bring to bear upon this corpus all these theories at once (and not merely one or the other). This demands several interrelated levels of analysis that he briefly illustrates in this essay, and which allow him to progress systematically from the surface organization of the legal argument to its symbolic function, and, in the process, to elucidate characteristics of the Jewish legal/ethical discourse. Yet, Haas's proposal is also pioneering in the sense that he needs to devise a methodology for the study of legal discourse (in general). Indeed, as the diversity of his methodological sources shows, there is no ready-made methodology for this kind of study. Thus he had to become involved in the field of theoretical research about "how legal discourse (in general) functions," so as to help develop the theory upon which a sound methodology could be based, constantly making sure that the theory and the methodology apply adequately to the Jewish legal corpus (and, more specifically to the *Responsa,* an ideal test case). By confronting theories about legal discourse to the responsa, he contributes to the elaboration of these theories; a general theory of legal discourse needs to be able to account for all types of legal discourses, including *Jewish* legal discourses.

Since semiotics is a research field aiming at developing a theory accounting for meaning in any discourse (and signifying phenomenon) by constantly confronting its model to new corpora which raise new questions, it is clear that the semioticians have much to learn from Haas's work. It demands that they reconsider semiotic theory so as to make sure that it can account for the characteristics of legal discourse and ethics and, more specifically, of Jewish legal discourse and ethics. In turn, semiotics might provide some insights which could help the research on legal discourse and ethics to progress, and thus help develop analytical/exegetical methods which could apply to any (not merely Jewish) ethical discourse; such methods are much needed in biblical studies (and especially, in my field, New Testament studies).

The fact that the Jewish ethical corpus is a corpus of legal discourses throws a peculiar light on the phenomenon "ethics," that we define broadly as the process through which decisions affecting one's behavior are made (a process which can be described semiotically, since it is a "signifying" process). At the outset, the Jewish corpus as discussed by Haas suggests that any decision-making should be viewed as somewhat similar to a legal argument, and that it always involves something like a "law." This can be understood when one notes that making a decision is truly needed only "when two apparently irreconcilable demands come into conflict," the very situation which Haas describes as prompting a responsum (and, more generally, a legal argument). Thus, the categories Haas uses should help us better understand the phenomenon of ethics.

Yet this form of the Jewish ethical discourse also suggests that there is something specific about Jewish ethics which demands that it be expressed in the form of legal discourse, rather than in another form of decision-making. Haas's proposal that Jewish ethics takes the form of legal discourse because it appeals to the Sinai/Torah myth which posits a "cosmic structure" characterized by a legal form, is certainly moving in the right direction. Yet this proposal (in part III of this essay) comes somewhat as a surprise for the reader. One is then led to raise the question: what is its relation with the preceding discussion and analysis of the legal argument in terms of various categories?

A review of the categories Haas found useful in describing the legal discourse of the responsa is therefore in order so as to try to perceive how they could help us better understand Haas's proposal concerning the legal form of Jewish ethics, and eventually refine it. For someone trained in semiotics, it quickly appears that these categories correspond to certain "dimensions of meaning" that semiotics recognizes in any signifying phenomenon (discourse, behavior, etc.), dimensions of meaning that semiotics strives to identify more precisely so as to understand their places and roles in making this phenomenon "meaningful." Looking at these categories from this semiotic perspective helps both clarify the contribution of Haas's essay and refine the semiotic theory in light of his research. Because of space limitations, we cannot present here the far-reaching implications of Haas's work for a semiotics of ethical discourse. We will primarily be concerned to specify the status of the "law" and of the "legal form" in Jewish ethical discourses, in an attempt to clarify further what, in Judaism, requires that the ethical discourse take a legal form.

  A. Haas distinguishes, following Ladd, "what people claim they should or should not do" from "the values and beliefs" which are "the linguistic universe in which a culture's moral discourse takes place." This distinction—which applies to any ethical discourse—corresponds to the one made in semiotics between "syntax" (in the case of moral/legal discourses, the logical syntax which is the argumentative concatenation of points through which we express what we should or should not do) and "semantics" (in the specific sense of the holistic *system* of convictions, values, and symbols which forms the "universe" in which our moral/legal discourse takes place, called in semiotics a "semantic universe," a concept broader than "linguistic universe"). This first distinction is essential because without it, as Haas expressed in his own words, one could be misled into thinking that "what people claim" (the syntax) is the entire meaning of a moral/legal discourse. In fact, such a claim would be meaningless if it was not taking place in a semantic universe. Conversely, a semantic universe (one's convictions, values, symbolism) needs to find expression in a syntax, otherwise it remains a pure virtuality; it would not truly be the semantic universe of the people involved in the moral/legal discourse. Yet, as Haas would agree, the semantic universe is primary; as the universe in which a meaningful discourse unfolds, it imposes constraints upon the syntax or, more specifically, upon the form the syntax can take.

  B. In a legal system, Haas distinguishes, following Hart, "primary rules" (overt regulations) from "secondary rules" (the procedures and norms upon which the primary rules are based). We can relate this distinction to the preceding one by noting that a legal system is, insofar as it is accepted, what people in a society (or group) view as expressing "what they should or should not do." In other words, in view of the preceding observations, a *legal system, the law, is syntactic* in nature, and *not* semantic. This remark suggests that Haas's proposal involves a confusion of syntax and semantics. According to him the convictions (semantic universe), which give to the Jewish moral discourse its legal form, is a Sinai/Torah myth (a system of convictions) which has a legal form ("the giving of the law at Sinai"). Indeed, the Sinai/Torah myth has a syntactical expression ("the giving of the law at Sinai," a legal form). It is also true that the Jewish moral discourse replicates the syntactical form of the myth ("rabbinic legal activity, then, is understood to be a continuation of that seminal act at Sinai"). Yet these insightful observations still do not elucidate the "basic religious convictions" that both that myth and the Jewish legal discourse embody in their syntactical expressions.

We also need to note that this second distinction emphasizes that the legal system (as "what people claim they should or should not do") is a consensus, i.e., the expression of what the speaker/author and the audience should (hopefully) agree upon. In terms of moral/legal discourses, this is a dimension of the meaning of the argument that the speaker assumes the audience will readily accept, a feature of what is called in semiotics "discursive syntax" (the syntax as establishing the speaker and the audience in a successful discursive communication). In it one needs to distinguish two dimensions: the main argument (the "primary rules") and the warrants of this argument (the "secondary rules"). As Haas notes, and as semiotics has also found, this distinction is important when one wants to elucidate the "semantics" which finds expression and undergirds a legal system (and any discursive syntax). It is the warrants (the "secondary rules"), and not the main argument (the "primary rules"), which are the most direct expression of the main convictions and values that define a "society's notion of good and evil" (what semiotics calls "discursive semantics"). These remarks, prompted by Haas's work, help us understand the dimension of meaning to which "laws" belong, namely, discursive syntax as expression of a discursive semantics, a point which semiotics needed to see clarified.

C. Following Perelman and his view of legal discourse as a kind of syllogism, Haas further distinguishes between, on the one hand, the *major normative premise* which "asserts some good which the law is meant to establish," and, on the other hand, the *minor premise* which is the particular interpretation given to the issue at hand, an interpretation which predetermines the judicial decision (which then "appears to flow logically"). This distinction is related to the preceding one but goes one step further. In the argument (the syntax), it distinguishes, on the one hand, what belongs to the consensus between speaker and audience (the discursive syntax), namely, the major normative premise as reexpression of aspects of the law, and, on the other hand, the creative contribution of the speaker (judge), namely, the minor premise. While the major premise is "subjective" (as Haas says) in the sense that the judge chooses it, and while the minor premise (the interpretation of the issue at hand) is expressed in such a way as to be acceptable to the audience, it remains that the minor premise is a primary expression of the speaker's (judge's) view. This distinction allows, therefore, envisioning another level of the syntax, that level which expresses the speaker's creativity, his/her own ideas and moral values (views of what one should or should not do), that is, what Greimas calls the "semio-narrative syntax" (using a vocabulary which betrays the fact that he started his research on narratives). This distinction is important when one wants to elucidate, as Haas wants to do, "the broader system of convictions out of which the responsum grows," that is, "the consensus of the (Jewish) culture." One should avoid confusing the idiosyncrasies of an author (judge) with this consensus. In practical terms, it means that the minor premises should be handled with great care in the analysis, since they are heavily loaded with the speaker's personal views and perspectives.

D. Following Dworkin, Haas makes a distinction between the "values and beliefs" which belong to the judge (or speaker), the judge's "taste and judgment" (on the basis of which is determined what the law should do), and the "values and principles" which are assumed to be accepted as self-evident by the intended audience. This distinction is similar to the preceding one, although it now distinguishes *two* "*semantic*" *levels* (instead of two syntactic levels); on the one hand, the "consensus" or *discursive semantic* system, i.e., the convictions and values which the judge and the audience share; and on the other hand, the *semio-narrative semantic* system, the judge's *taste*, his/her own system of convictions (or micro-semantic universe).

Granted the judge's or rabbi's convictions (most directly expressed in syntactical form in the minor premise) and the shared convictions (most directly expressed in a syntactical form by the legal system and the major premise) necessarily overlap, but one cannot simply identify them, as Haas tends to do. Otherwise it would be useless for the people to go to a rabbi; if the rabbi's system of convictions were the same as theirs, he would not be able to help them resolve the tension between what they perceive as two irreconcilable demands.

In order to understand the respective roles of these two semantic systems (the system of convictions of the rabbi, and that of the people) in a responsum (or legal argument), let us consider how the need for such a responsum arises. People have a semantic universe (convictions, values) which finds expression in the law that spells out what they should or should not do. Yet they are confronted by a new situation such that they cannot ignore it (an existential situation, in the sense that it is an integral part of their existence). Now this situation poses for them self-evident truths (convictions, values) which are in tension with those of their original semantic universe (expressed by the law). As a consequence, they find themselves with a divided semantic universe, or better with two (partial) semantic universes in tension and on the basis of which two conflicting kinds of behavior are envisioned (the potential syntactic expression of these semantic universes); what they should or should not do according to the convictions expressed in the law is in tension with what they should or should not do according to the self-evident truths posited by the existential situation. On the other hand, the rabbi also has a semantic universe which finds expression in the law, but in his case this semantic universe is, so to speak, "larger" in that it can integrate the new existential situation and the self-evident truths it poses. In other words, for the rabbi, the self-evident truths posed by the new situation (the feeling of pity according to which people should not suffer excruciating pain when there is no hope for relief and survival) are perceived as congruent with his original convictions and thus can find their place in his system of convictions.

The point of these comments is that a legal argument (and for that matter any moral discourse) is not the mere resolution of a practical problem (what one should or should not do in a specific situation, a syntactic problem) through the correct application of shared convictions. It will only bring this resolution insofar as it first transforms the system of convictions of the audience. We can go as far as saying that a moral problem, despite its syntactic formulation in terms of what one should or should not do, is always fundamentally a semantic problem; it arises from a "deficiency" in the audience's (or a person's) system of convictions. In the case of the responsum, note that the people who ask the question are devoted to the law; but they are unable to interpret it appropriately in the new situation. In other words, they know and accept the "primary rules," but do not know the appropriate norms and principles (the "secondary rules") that allow the application of the primary rules to the new situation. Now, as we have noted, these secondary rules are the most directly related to basic convictions. Thus, their problem arises from a "deficiency" in the basic convictions concerning the fundamental character of the law, indeed in the convictions which give rise to the law (or, more generally, to moral imperatives, in the case of other moral discourses).

It appears, therefore, that by identifying in the Jewish legal discourse the way in which the rabbi strives to transform the convictions of the intended audience, one would be in a position to elucidate the most characteristic (and fundamental) convictions in Jewish ethics, indeed those which demand that the Jewish ethical discourse take a legal form. I believe Haas's essay contains observations which suggest what these basic convictions could be, although he does not spell them out.

In the case at hand, Haas notes that Palaggi "simply assumes the legal and moral imperative to relieve pain." Two observations are in order. First, the imperative to relieve the dying person's excruciating pain arises from the confrontation of people with the concrete situation; its convictional basis is a "feeling" of pity, the spontaneous (self-evident) perception that such a situation is bad (or evil), what we can call, using Greimas's terminology, a *"thymic"* conviction, i.e., a conviction concerning the "quality" of the life-situation in which one is, and the "mood" resulting from the perception of (moral or aesthetic) values in it. This second observation follows from the first: such "thymic" convictions make up what Geertz calls *"ethos"* (note that the above explanation of "thymic conviction" is basically the same as Geertz's explanation of "ethos"). Furthermore, Geertz distinguishes "ethos" from "world-view," that he defines as "the picture (people) have of the way things in sheer actuality are." Using Greimas's terminology, we can say that a "world-view" is made up of *"veridictory"* convictions (what is self-evidently perceived as "truly being").

Coming back to Palaggi's responsum, we can thus note that by assuming the imperative of relieving pain, he recognizes as self-evidently valid the "thymic conviction" which arose in the concrete situation. This suggests that, for him, "thymic convictions" would be the most fundamental (they cannot be discussed or questioned), and consequently that "veridictory convictions" would be less fundamental.

Of course, such a suggestion should be verified by an analysis of the responsum aimed at distinguishing the respective roles of "thymic" and "veridictory" convictions, or, and this amounts to the same thing, of the "ethos" and the "world-view." Obviously, such an analysis cannot be done here. Yet, a few additional (and concluding) remarks seem to support this suggestion.

Any system of convictions (semantic universe) involves an "ethos" and a "world-view." Geertz presupposes that the overall organization of a system of convictions is provided by the "world-view" (since he says that it is for the people "their most comprehensive ideas of order"). This is certainly true in many cosmological and western cultures. In such a case, the hierarchic organization of the system of convictions (the "world-view" and its "veridictory" convictions being primary, and the "ethos" and its "thymic" convictions being secondary) leads to the common moral discourses which base arguments about decision-making (the syntactic expression of the ethos) upon theological or metaphysical arguments (the syntactical expression of the world-view). But, as is well known and further shown by Haas's work, Jewish ethical discourse is not based upon a theological argument; this is what gives it a purely legal character. This could be understood if indeed the Jewish system of convictions received its overall organization from its "ethos" and "thymic" convictions, rather than from its "world-view" and "veridictory" convictions. In such a case, the ethical discourse can take the syntactic form of a purely legal discourse, which can stand on its own (without the help of a theological discourse). In fact, in such a case, theological arguments would need to be based upon ethical/legal arguments, which seems to be the case in the early Jewish literature.

These suggestions, if they are verified, could open a way of pursuing the research on Jewish ethics beyond Haas's essay. But, obviously, they are not to be taken as a negative critique of Haas's work; indeed, without his excellent pioneering work, these suggestions could not even be conceived.

JEWISH LEGAL INTERPRETATION: LITERARY, SCRIPTURAL, SOCIAL, AND ETHICAL PERSPECTIVES[1]

David Ellenson
Hebrew Union College, Los Angeles

ABSTRACT

Moral decisions in Judaism occur when specific texts are brought to bear in specific contexts. This proposition is explored in the following essay. Again attention focusses on a responsum, this time by the late nineteenth century Orthodox rabbi Solomon Kluger. He is asked about the acceptability of Passover Matzah (unleavened bread) made by machine. His answer, that we are not to use such matzah, is ostensibly based on the received texts of the tradition. But Ellenson shows that contemporary social and economic issues are also at stake. A step by step analysis of Kluger's argument shows that Jewish ethics is always text-focussed. Yet this fact means that multiple interpretations are always possible. The choice as to which interpretation is correct is linked to social, historical and/or psychological factors.

A translation of the responsum considered here follows this essay.

The liturgy of the Synagogue expresses the reverence Judaism holds for Jewish sacred scriptures when, in the words of a daily evening prayer, it states of them, "For they are our life and the length of our days, and upon them we will meditate day and night." The holy texts of Judaism—both Written Law (biblical) and Oral Law (rabbinic)—are seen as divine in origin and timeless in their import and meaning. Their messages are viewed as comprehensive and valid, guiding and normative forever. Commitment to these texts, and to the elucidation of their meanings, ensures that they will be dealt with exegetically ever anew—albeit that the interpretations such efforts yield are said to be contained in God's original Sinaitic revelation.[2] Jewish tradition expresses this paradox concerning the comprehensive nature of Torah in the statement of a *tannaitic* (early rabbinic authority of the first two centuries of the Common Era) authority, who is reported to have said of Torah, "Turn its pages over and over again, for all is in it" (*Pirkei Avot* 5:25). The hermeneutical task—the goal of permitting the texts to speak and, thereby, be enduringly relevant to every generation—is thus one which has confronted the believing Jew and one in which the believing Jew has engaged for over two millenia.

This exegetical challenge has been met in Judaism not only through commentaries upon the Written Law, but through the development of the Oral Law as well. Central to this development for over a thousand years has been the genre of rabbinic literature known as *She'elot u 'Teshuvot* (Questions and Answers—Responsa), in which leading rabbinic jurist-legislators have issued authoritative renderings *(piskei din)* of Jewish Law *(Halakha)* to rabbinic colleagues for application and, sometimes, public dissemination in specific cases. Responsa are thus elite, technical documents—case discussions and their "holdings" in modern Western jurisprudential nomenclature—and rabbis throughout the centuries have used them to apply the insights, meanings, norms, and precedents provided by the literary and legal texts of the Jewish past (Bible, Talmud, Codes, and other responsa) to the pressing and often novel issues of the present age. Consequently, a single responsum must be seen as part of a vast body of Jewish case law which stretches over the centuries. *It is the crossroads where text and context meet in the ongoing tradition of Jewish legal hermeneutics.* As such, each responsum is an autonomous text, to be analyzed synchronically, written in a particular milieu by a specific author. However, and equally important, each should also be viewed diachronically as an individual reflection of a continuous body of Jewish literature with its own style, language, and logic. These idiomatic expressions of Jewish thought therefore provide an excellent lens through which to witness the role of the classical Jewish literary tradition (Bible, Talmud, and occasionally Midrash) and later rabbinic texts (Codes, Responsa, and occasionally Commentaries and philosophical literature), as well as the input of contemporary social, psychological, and ethical factors, in the development of Judaism.

The author of the responsum chosen for analysis and discussion in this essay is Solomon Kluger (1763–1869) of Brody, a prominent Galician Orthodox rabbi. Kluger played an active role in the guidance of Jewish communal affairs in Eastern and Central Europe and Orthodox rabbis throughout these regions frequently turned to him for advice. One of the most prolific authors of responsa in history, Kluger published literally thousands of opinions. All of them, including the one under consideration here, are written in classical rabbinic language and style, and they serve as models for this type of scholarship. As such, they reveal the role that text and tradition assume in this mode of Jewish legal writing. On the other hand, Kluger's responsa bespeak a man deeply embroiled in the European Jewish world of the 1800's. Keenly aware of the social, scientific, and religious transformations the nineteenth century brought to European Jewish life, Kluger, in this as well as his other responsa, becomes paradigmatic of the contemporary religious authority struggling to adjust—either through resistance or compromise—to the realities created by a new age. Consequently, his legal opinions indicate the significance that must be assigned the contemporary milieu in assaying the nature of the responsa literature.[3]

The particular responsum selected for discussion in his essay is the first in a collection of responsa Rabbi Kluger published under the title, *Moda'ah l'Beit Yisrael (Announcement to the Household of Israel)*, in Breslau in 1859. The responsa in this volume deal with the question of whether it is permissible to use machine-baked *matzot* (unleavened bread) during the Passover festival.[4] Traditionally, of course, all *matzot* were baked entirely by hand. However, in Austria in 1857 a machine was invented for this purpose. Its use quickly spread to other countries, especially Germany—the birthplace of both Reform Judaism and a modern Jewish Orthodoxy receptive to contemporary cultural currents. Indeed, the pace of Jewish acculturation in Germany, even among the Orthodox, caused Eastern European Orthodox rabbis like Kluger to view German Jewry with suspicion and made them hesitant to depend upon German-Jewish innovations (such as machine-baked *matzot*) in religious customs as authoritative for their own practices. This point is significant, as it contributes an important context for understanding the Kluger responsum analyzed in this paper. For, as we shall see, Kluger opposed this departure from traditional European Jewish religious practice, in part, on these grounds.

The responsum itself is addressed to Rabbis Hayyim Nathan and Lebush Horowitz of Cracow, and the arguments Kluger advances in this document are the first to protest this particular change in European Jewish life. As an aside, it is interesting to note that Kluger's positions, as put forth in this responsum, became the basis for Jewish legal arguments against the employment of this machine among those rabbis who opposed machine-baked *matzot* for Passover usage.[5] Indeed, this clearly testifies both to Kluger's mastery of traditional rabbinic literature and his influence on the Orthodox rabbinic world of the nineteenth century. In sum, this responsum embodies a number of literary, legal, social, and historical features essential to a discussion and analysis of this form of Jewish legal literature.

This paper, through such discussion and analysis, will provide the reader with an understanding of the nature of the responsa literature and delineate several possibilities for future research in this field. It will do this by exploring four areas. The first, a literary one, will simply outline the form of the responsum so that the reader will grasp the nature and role of literary structure in the responsa. An explication of the statutory position Bible and Talmud occupy and the precedential purpose codes, commentaries, and other responsa serve in this literature will then be offered. In this way the place of Scripture in the millennium old tradition of Jewish case law will be highlighted and the semi-autonomous nature of Jewish legal method will be illuminated. However, because responsa are not issued in a vacuum, but are the products of particular authors writing at a specific time, the social-historical context of the document must be considered. By viewing the Kluger responsum in this manner, another way of understanding the interpretations and decisions advanced in the responsa can be gained.[6] Finally, as the point is often made that the *Halakhah* represents the "concretization" of Jewish values,[7] this paper will consider the role of ethics in Kluger's responsum and, in so doing, show how a responsum can be employed to adduce something about the nature of the relationship between law and morality in Judaism. Through such an examination and analysis of the Kluger responsum, this paper will both introduce the reader to the responsa literature and provide insights into the nature of Judaism itself.

i

The Kluger responsum, representative as it is of this genre of Jewish legal literature, follows a uniform literary structure that marks the responsa literature. For despite regional differences which may have characterized the formal conventions of the responsum in earlier historical epochs, the responsa had come to assume a standard literary style long before Kluger authored his opinions in the nineteenth century. Indeed, these uniformities of style, structure, and convention combine to make the responsa a distinctive and easily identifiable type of literature.

In form, Kluger's responsum, like others of this genre, is an epistle. However, as an epistle, it is vital to note that it is also a legal instrument. The employment of this epistolary style for a legal document is certainly medieval in origin, as it was a common convention in the Middle Ages to utilize letters as legal devices (e.g., papal bulls and royal decrees in Christian Europe and the *fatwa* in the Islamic world).[8] Thus, the Kluger responsum begins with an identification of the author and the addressees, which includes a *captatio benevolentiae,* or flourish, designed to flatter and signify the importance of the addressees. This "honorific apostrophe," hyperbolic and ornamental in tone, is a standard literary device employed in virtually all responsa. In addition, the date and place of origin is cited at the beginning of the responsum. Again, this is a common hallmark of the responsa literature, though other writers of this legal genre will place the date and locale at the end, not at the beginning, of their responsa.[9]

It is in the *corpus* of the responsum that narration of the issue begins. In this instance, Kluger himself relates the issue in a summary, declarative form, though, in other cases, the matter may be put forth in an interrogatory style. The reader is now aware that a discussion of legal precedents and sources relevant to the disposition of this particular matter is about to ensue. Consequently, throughout the body of the responsum, Kluger cites and analyzes biblical sources of Jewish law (e.g., the reading of the *Megillah* on Purim), numerous passages from the Talmud (e.g., *BT Megillah* 4b and *BT Pesachim* 36–37), later medieval rabbinic authorities (*Rishonim* and the Tosafists), and Codes (e.g., *Tur, Shulchan Aruch* and the *Shulchan Aruch*) to arrive at and buttress his decision in this matter. In addition, where disputes might arise about the proper exegesis of one of these sources (e.g., the penultimate paragraph of the responsum), Kluger offers a resolution to the difficulty so that a definitive ruling may emerge from the source in question. Following this discussion and analysis, Kluger is able to render a decision in the matter before him. Thus, he concludes, "It is proper to say that all *matzot* which are not made by an adult Jewish man are forbidden, and God forbid that one should assert that those made by a machine are permissible for use." With this final declaration, the *corpus* of the responsum is completed, the classical literary structure of this section of the responsum (citation and discussion of relevant sources, resolution of difficulties in the sources, and final decision) having been observed.

The *eschatocol* (concluding section) of the responsum now proceeds in a fashion that leaves no doubt that the communication is over. The moral and religious exhortations ("Therefore, do not veer from the customs of your fathers. . . .) in the final paragraph, the protestation of weakness and humility, and the signature of the author indicate that the responsum is concluded in a standard rabbinic legal form.

In addition to the literary conventions already cited, it is significant to point out that Kluger employs a typical rabbinic diction. The language of the responsum is Hebrew with a smattering of rabbinic Aramaic, and the linguistic style itself is rabbinic-Talmudic. These factors clearly testify to the elements of continuity between this literature and the classical sources of Judaism. Morever, this choice of language and style, as well as the formal literary conventions of the Kluger responsum, are all paradigmatic characteristics of the responsa literature from the early Middle Ages to the present day, and they combine to identify this document as a "normative" one within this area of Jewish jurisprudence. These accepted patterns of literary structure and diction, far from being incidental to the responsum, are thus critical in establishing Kluger's, or any other rabbinic author's, credibility within this chain of Jewish legal tradition. As such, the form of the responsum—its style, language, and conventions—is an essential part of the authoritative posture a rabbi assumes in rendering a legal decision to his colleagues. Knowledge of the literary components of the responsa consequently provide a valuable means for comprehending and identifying the meanings and messages of this literature.

ii

The responsa, as mentioned above, are, in fact, judicial opinions issued by legal authorities in specific cases. The issue of legal hermeneutics is thus one that cannot be avoided in dealing with these texts. For each responsum, as part of a mature legal system that stretches back over a thousand years, claims to be an authoritative rendering and/or application of Jewish sacred texts and the principles derived from these texts to the problems of a contemporary situation.

The Jewish legal system, in making such claims, is not unique. Indeed, the legal exegesis evidenced in the responsa literature is comparable to the process of legal reasoning that takes place in other systems of law. This process, as David A. J. Richards has observed, displays two major characteristics. The first is that the decisor, or judge, "infers the legal standards applicable to a particular situation from (a) body of so-called primary authority."[10] In American law this "body of so-called primary authority" includes both the Constitution, which assumes a "statutory" role in the American legal system, and an ongoing process of judicial opinions which function in a "precedential" way. Here the interpretation of the law offered in a previous case (its *holding*) is seen to have a bearing on the adjudication of a contemporary case dealing with the same issue of law. A second feature of legal reasoning, related to but not identical with the first, is that of "reasoning by analogy." The court, in this instance, not only takes prior holdings on a comparable issue into account when rendering its decision, but extends "principles of law found applicable to one set of fact patterns . . . to other fact patterns which are in relevant respects similar."[11]

The Kluger responsum, representative as it is of this genre of Jewish legal literature, evidences both these traits. The statutory role occupied by Bible and Talmud in the Jewish legal system is obvious throughout the responsum. Indeed, the obligation to eat the *matzah* of commandment on the first night of Passover, which undergirds the discussion in the last three-quarters of the responsum, is derived from *Exodus* 12:18 ("In the first month on the fourteenth day of the month *at evening*, you shall eat unleavened bread . . .") and the Talmudic exegesis of that passage in the Bible, located in *BT Pesachim* 120a. Interestingly, however, these statutory passages are not even cited in the Kluger text. This is because Kluger, writing as he is to rabbinical colleagues, assumes their knowledge of these scriptural verses, thus obviating the need to cite them directly. The elite, technical nature of this literature, as well as the statutory status of Bible and Talmud in it, is revealed in this manner. Furthermore, Kluger bases his opposition to the use of machine-baked *matzot* on Passover upon passages in the Babylonian Talmud (*Pesachim* 36b and 37a) which detail some of the supervisory requirements that must be fulfilled if *matzah* which is ritually fit for consumption on the first night of Passover is to be baked. As *matzah* produced by a machine—in contrast to that made by hand—could not, in Kluger's opinion, meet those Talmudic standards of "strict and careful supervision," it was to be prohibited. The correctness of Kluger's readings of these texts aside, the crucial point to be made here is that Kluger arrives at his decision on the basis of his citations and interpretations of these "statutory" Jewish legal texts.

Moreover, Kluger, in issuing his opinion, also relies upon "precedential" literature found in the Jewish legal tradition. This literature, seen as authoritative in its own right, allows Kluger to cite, among others, the teachings and rulings of the early medieval rabbinic authorities (the *Rishonim*), the French and German medieval commentators upon the Talmud (the Tosafists), the *Tur, Sulchan Aruch* (the law code of Rabbi Jacob ben Asher, 1270–1340), and the *Shulchan Aruch* (the great legal code of Joseph Caro, 1564) in arriving at his decision. His efforts in this direction also permit the reader to see precisely how it is that a later court is, in some sense, always engaged in a process of interpretation and reformulation concerning the law itself. This is because the legal process, by its very nature, is a dynamic one which requires the later court, through its ruling, to both determine what the actual holding was in a previous case as well as the weight to be assigned that holding in determining the contemporary one. Thus, in the penultimate paragraph of his responsum, Kluger notes that the *Tur, Shulchan Aruch* holds, "All Syrian cakes are forbidden, whether those of bakers or of private persons." The cause for concern regarding such "cakes" is revealed in the Talmudic passage referred to by Kluger himself. There, in *TB Pesachim* 37a, it states:

> Rab Judah said: This thing Boethus b. Zonin asked the Sages: Why was it said that Syrian cakes shaped in figures must not be made on Passover? Said they to him, Because a woman would tarry over it and cause it to turn to leaven. . . .

This fear that there would be a delay in the baking, and that the "cakes" would subsequently rise and leaven, led the rabbis of the Talmud immediately to the following story. The passage in *Pesachim* thus continues:

> R. Eleazar b. Zadok said: I once followed my father into the house of R. Gamaliel, and they placed before him Syrian cakes shaped in figures on

Passover. Said I, 'Father, did not the Sages say thus, One may not make Syrian cakes shaped in figures on Passover'? 'My son,' he replied, 'they did not speak of (the cakes of) all people, but only those of bakers' (Note—who bake for sale. They are more particular for the shape to be exactly right and so may take too long over it. But private people are not so particular.). Others say, he said thus to him: 'They did not speak of those of bakers, but (only) of those of private people.'

Thus, in the Talmud, the issue remains unresolved. Some authorities might assert, on the basis of one statement, that "only (the cakes) of bakers" are forbidden. However, others might contend, on the strength of the final statement, that those of bakers are permitted, but that "those of private people" are forbidden. It is for this reason that Kluger, quite correctly, observes that "there is a dispute among the rabbinic authorities" of Talmudic times on this matter. Nevertheless, for our purposes it is critical to note 1) that the *Tur, Shulchan Aruch* resolves the dispute, forbidding Syrian cakes produced by bakers and private persons alike, 2) that Kluger accepts Jacob ben Asher's resolution of the dispute as authoritative, and 3) that Kluger assigns this later, precedential holding weight in issuing his ruling in the case before him. While the earlier, "statutory" text (the Talmud) is theoretically more authoritative than the later, "precedential" code (the *Tur*), in reality the "precedent," i.e., the ruling of the *Tur*, defines the meaning of the "statutory" text, i.e., the Talmud. To assert on this basis, however, that fidelity to the Talmud as the source for Jewish law is cast aside would be misleading. Rather, this example demonstrates that in Jewish law, as in many other legal systems, a later interpretation of a "statutory" text earns a precedential status because it claims to embody the legitimate reading of the earlier text. Moreover, in so doing it clarifies the purpose and meaning of the statutory text itself. It is in this way that the later text assumes a weight of its own in the legal system, albeit that it would claim nothing novel for itself. The process of Jewish law as reflected in this use of "statutory" and "precedential" texts thus clearly conforms to the first major feature, that of inferring "legal standards to a particular situation from (a) body of so-called primary authority," which Richards sees as characterizing "the process of legal reasoning."

The second feature, that of "reasoning by analogy," reveals once more the text-centered nature of Jewish law and is evidenced at the very outset of Kluger's opinion. Here Kluger cites *BT Megillah* 4b, which holds unequivocally that the Purim reading of the *Book of Esther* is not to take place on the Sabbath. The reason for this is that *matanot l'evyonim*, "gifts to the poor," are dispensed to indigent members of the community, in accordance with *Esther* 10:22, immediately after the reading of the Scroll, "and on the Sabbath these could not be given."[12] The principle of public policy established here, i.e., concern for the poor, is deemed relevant by Kluger to the case before him. For if *machine-baked* matzot are permitted for Passover use, then all the poor workers traditionally engaged in the enterprise of baking *matzot* by hand would be left unemployed, though they "anxiously await this (task) in order to earn wages for Passover" necessities. While the moral considerations evidenced here will be discussed below, the item of note at this juncture is that Kluger applies "principles of law found applicable to one set of fact patterns . . . to other fact patterns which are in relevant respects similar." Just as the Talmudic rabbis forbade the reading of the *Megillah* on the Sabbath out of concern for the poor, so Kluger would forbid the utilization of a machine for the baking of *matzot* because of the untoward economic consequences it would have for the needy.

In sum, an analysis of the Kluger responsum demonstrates that Jewish law is text-focused. The decision rendered in a responsum, to be authoritative, must justify itself explicitly in terms of either a principle or a text found in the Bible/Talmud or later rabbinic tradition. The responsum's conformity to these canons of legal reasoning bespeaks the integrity and semi-autonomous nature of the process of Jewish law, and a sensitivity to this process heightens the reader's awareness of the responsum as part of a legal, and not just religious and/or moral system. Moreover, it is this legal context which must be kept uppermost in mind in comprehending and appreciating the nature of this literature.

iii

The Jewish legal tradition, as indicated above, possesses an integrity of its own. Kluger or any other respondent, must, if he wishes his responsum to be accepted as authoritative, defend his interpretation of the Law in light of the texts of the Jewish tradition. His opinion must be unimpeachable from a textual perspective. Indeed, the biography and historical context in which the author lived is not a substitute for analyzing the style, logic, and canons of jurisprudence the legal author employed in the writing of his responsum.

This should not obscure the fact, however, that an exclusive focus on the literary and legal features of a Jewish legal opinion would ultimately be distorting if a fuller comprehension of the responsum would be attained. For Jewish law, like law in other systems, is not totally self-contained. Texts do not produce a univocal reading. Rather, in the hands of different interpreters, conclusions can be drawn in a variety of ways. Moreover, there can often be disagreements in the Jewish legal tradition—again as in other such traditions—as to the "right" a specific text has to be "heard" in a given case. One rabbi, in rendering a decision, will cite a certain text in support of his opinion, while a second rabbinic authority will deem that text irrelevant in arriving at a decision on the same matter. An examination of the social-historical context in which a rabbi authored a responsum, as well as an investigation into the personality and psychology of the decisor, will aid in understanding the motivations and stimuli which led a rabbinic authority to issue a specific judgment in a given case. A probing of several aspects of the Kluger responsum will illustrate the nature of these observations.

Kluger, in arriving at his conclusion that ". . . it certainly is not permissible to fulfill one's obligation concerning the consumption of *matzah* on Passover through those produced by a machine," bases it, in part, on the contention that ". . . the Law has established for us the ruling that one is not exempt from fulfilling this commandment if a deaf-mute, an idiot, or a child produces it (the *matzah*), as none of them are mentally competent." This "Law" is contained in a passage of the *Shulchan Aruch,* which states, "One neither kneads (the dough necessary) for the *matzah* of commandment nor bakes it . . . under the supervision of a deaf-mute, an idiot, or a child" (Orach Hayyim 460:1). On the basis of this passage, as well as later rabbinic exegesis upon it, Kluger continues by pointing out that an adult, intelligent Jew must literally participate in and supervise the baking of the *matzot* from the moment the flour is kneaded until the *matzah* itself is finally baked. As *matzah* produced by a machine, which has no intelligence, could not fulfill this criterion, machine-baked *matzot* are by definition not ritually fit to be eaten on the first night of Passover. On the other hand, Joseph Saul Nathanson (1810–1875), Rabbi of Lemberg, in his *Bittul Moda'ah (Annulment of the Announcement),* published in 1859 as both a response and refutation of Kluger, claims that this text, and the exegesis which flows from it, does not disqualify the machine for use in the baking of ritually acceptable *matzot* on Passover. As the machine is operated by an "intelligent person," this dispenses altogether, in Nathanson's view, with the issue of the machine's "mental competence." It simply becomes an irrelevancy. Moreover, the real intent of the *Orach Hayyim* passage, Nathanson contends, is to emphasize the need for constant and strict supervision in both the preparation and baking of the *matzot,* so as to guard against the danger of the dough's leavening. Yet, the possibility of this happening is lessened, not heightened, by the employment of the machine. For the machine works more rapidly than many persons, thus reducing the chances that the dough might rise in the baking process. In short, Nathanson reads the same text differently than Kluger, utilizing it to justify the use of the machine for the baking of *matzot* on the eve of Passover.[13]

In addition, Kluger, reasoning by analogy, views the text in *BT Megillah* 4b as providing a decisive argument against the utilization of machine-baked *matzot* during Passover. His logic for employing that text in this fashion has been discussed in the preceding section. What is of interest here is that Nathanson, in the same responsum noted above, states that the *Megillah* text cited by Kluger is totally irrelevant to the question before them, claiming that the issue is not one of providing for the poor on Passover, but of determining whether *matzah* produced by a machine is fit for ritual consumption on the holiday. As the two cases—the one under discussion and the one in *Megillah*—are, in Nathanson's opinion, dissimilar, he will not grant the "right" of the *Megillah* text to be "heard" on this matter.

The point, in citing these two examples in the preceding paragraphs, is not to determine whether Kluger or Nathanson is right. This can certainly be left to Jewish legal authorities. In addition, these examples neither demonstrate that a text necessarily possesses more than one inherent, objective meaning, nor that Kluger, or Nathanson, *purposefully* read these texts in light of certain contextual realities. However, they do demonstrate that a text, e.g., *Orach Hayyim* 460:1, can be read by two authorities in different ways and that these same authorities may disagree as to the applicability of a given text, e.g., *Megillah* 4b, in the adjudication of a contemporary case. Thus, a key to understanding the nature of these differences, as well as why an individual rabbi read the tradition in the manner that he did, may well lie in an investigation of the social/historical context in which the responsum was written and in an examination of the psychological profile of the individual decisor. For rabbis, like jurists in any system of law, "come to their questions with propensities to interpret matters leniently or stringently, and to emphasize some principles at the expense of others."[14] Indeed, this, in part, is precisely what has happened here. *To comprehend the Kluger responsum, and the way in which he has interpreted the holy texts of the Jewish legal tradition, it is vital to see it in its social, historical, and/or psychological contexts, as these provide important clues for apprehending the motives which may have caused Kluger to read these texts and render this decision in the form that he did.* To assert this is not to commit the genetic fallacy. It is to understand the text in other than a purely literary or exclusively jurisprudential way.

Turning then to Kluger himself, it is important to keep in mind that historians have labelled him "an extremist in his orthodoxy, vehemently opposing the *maskilim* (Jewish Enlighteners), whose influence was already making itself felt in Brody, and fighting against every endeavor to change the least important of religious customs prevalent in Eastern Europe."[15] Indeed, the truth of this observation appears to be borne out by an examination of several other responsa Kluger issued. In one case Kluger held that a woman who publicly violated the Sabbath was to be "treated as if she were a Gentile,"[16] while in another, highly revealing one, Kluger replies to a query posed him by Rabbi Jonah Ashkenazi of Presswork. In this instance, Ashkenazi asked whether it was permissible to learn German in order to pass a government-administered examination in that language. Such an examination was required of every candidate for the rabbinate, and failure to pass it meant that the individual could not serve as a communal rabbi. In responding, Kluger stated that the language itself was "hateful to him," as the study of German "leads almost inevitably to heresy." Indeed, many people proficient in German, even when they observed the Law, still had "heresy lurking in their hearts." Thus, Kluger wrote:

> It can be seen that the spirit of the Lord was in the Rabbis. They gazed by means of the holy spirit into those times when it was impossible to obtain a rabbinical position without seeking intimacy with the ruling powers in order to win their favor by studying their sciences. Consequently, the Rabbi says, "Hate the rabbinical office and seek no intimacy with the ruling powers." I advise you to refrain from it. Is the hand of the Lord powerless to help you to earn a living by other means?[17]

In short, Kluger was painfully aware of the changes that were beginning to transform the nature of traditional Jewish life in nineteenth century Europe and the assimilatory tendencies that were emerging as a result of these transformations.[18] Consequently, he was concerned to erect barriers against these changes and to maintain a sense of traditional Jewish boundaries. While his policy in this regard may or may not have been a prudential one, it certainly provides an indispensable key for grasping both his mindset and the world in which he lived. Representing an embattled position, Kluger was determined to preserve his brand of "authentic Judaism" against the onslaught of the modern world. He was, in Peter Berger's terminology, an advocate of "resistance," not "accommodation," to the demands of the larger Western world.[19]

This motive, which undoubtedly was a factor in explaining his rulings in the cases cited above, also clearly surfaces in the responsum under discussion in this paper. At the outset, Kluger maintains, "One does not learn from the Germans for several reasons." The major one, quite obviously, is that virtually all German Jews, who responded to the relentless pressures exerted upon them by modernity in a manner which enthusiastically affirmed the worth of Western culture[20] were, in this sense, an anathema to Kluger. Consequently, these German Jews could not possibly provide, in Kluger's opinion, a proper model for how Jewish life ought to be led in the contemporary period. Machine-baked *matzot* intended for Passover usage—inasmuch as they had been introduced originally in "the German states"—were thus simply another indication of German Jewry's unfortunate tendency to compromise the integrity of the Jewish religion in response to modern societal influences. For the German Jews, as Kluger observed them, will simply "do as their heart desires, as is their way." This trend toward laxity in religious observance and the disinclination to defend the "custom(s) of (the) fathers"—hallmarks, in Kluger's view, of German Judaism—caused Kluger to contrast himself, as well as the efforts beliefs of his followers, to those of the German Jews. As he writes at the conclusion of his responsum, "However, we will walk in the footsteps of our fathers and depart from them neither to the right nor to the left."

In sum, an awareness of the social-historical situation in which Kluger found himself and the psychological state he experienced as a result of that situation, clearly reveal that Kluger was predisposed to read the texts of the Jewish tradition on the matter before him in a manner which would allow him to rule negatively on the consumption of machine-baked *matzot* during Passover. This does not mean that his exegesis of the holy texts of the Jewish legal tradition on this matter was not a correct one. Nor does it indicate that his readings of these texts were in any way contrived. Rather, it demonstrates that the social, historical, and psychological contexts provide the student of the responsa literature with important signals for seeing the unconscious and, at times, conscious motives a rabbinic authority brings with him in arriving at a decision on the basis of certain texts. As a result, an awareness and analysis of these contexts allow the student a clearer understanding of the exegetical process which takes place in the continuous tradition of Jewish legal hermeneutics. It thus permits both a different perspective on the Kluger, or any other, responsum to surface and a deeper, more complex understanding of the Jewish legal process to emerge.

iv

Scholars of law have frequently noted that there is a close relationship between morality and legal reasoning. Richards, in writing on this phenomenon, has observed, "Legal reasoning . . . importantly draws upon and invokes principles which courts slowly develop through a long process of precedent and reasoning. These principles are often moral ones. . . . (Consequently), moral principles play a central role in legal reasoning."[21] It is hardly surprising, or unique, then, that the Jewish legal system, including the responsa, display the same characteristic of morality as do others. Indeed, it has often been argued that Jewish law elevates ethics to the status of law and that individual cases become specific opportunities for rabbis to operationalize the ethical values of the Jewish tradition by applying them to concrete matters. Steven Schwarzschild, for example, contends, "Equity is not a factor additional to the *jus strictum*, but a judgment procedure which makes sure that the application of the law in each individual case is proper (i.e., moral)."[22] Furthermore, Menachem Elon, in a less sweeping statement, echoes Schwarzschild's sentiments and, in speaking of the responsa literature, observes, "The respondant in his responsum . . . included the moral imperative—to the extent that it was involved in the question before (him)—as a part of (his) rulings."23 Finally, Shubert Spero, writing in the same vein, states, ". . . In the writings of the later commentators, and particularly in the responsa literature, we find a tendency to incorporate these 'extra-legal' considerations into the Halakhic process so that these moral imperatives become actionable by the courts."24

This ethical feature of Jewish law, of which all these men speak, is unmistakably revealed in the Kluger text. At the very outset of his responsum Kluger, in arguing against the employment of the machine, declares, "Behold, the reason for the prohibition against this appears first and foremost to be that it is not within the framework of the upright and the moral to plunder the poor who are anxiously awaiting the performance of this commandment. For from the assistance they provide in the baking of *matzot,* they have a significant source of income for the many Passover expenses which accrue to our people." Fearful that mechanization of the *matzah*-baking process would leave many poor unemployed, there is little doubt that moral considerations played a primary role in moving Kluger toward the decision he rendered. Indeed, the significance of moral concerns as an integral part of the Jewish legal process is further revealed in Kluger's chastisement of prosperous members of the community for their failure to observe the practice of *Me'ot Ḥitin* (a collection made before Passover to supply for the holiday needs of the poor). Their neglect of this commandment establishes, in Kluger's words, "a standard of idolatrous conduct."

In light of this, it is crucial to note that Kluger grounds his moral objection to the use of a machine for the production of Passover *matzot* in a text taken from the Babylonian Talmud (i.e., *Megillah* 4b). This is significant for several reasons. First, it indicates that the Talmud itself, the source of Jewish law, embodies moral concerns and makes them, in legal parlance, "actionable." Secondly, it reveals that such concerns are taken up by the Tradition and may be employed by later authorities as legitimate considerations in rendering a contemporary decision. Finally, Kluger's citation of the *Megillah* text as a warrant for his decision underscores the point that the Kluger responsum is part of what is essentially a legal, and not a moral, system. That is, Kluger can raise this moral consideration precisely because he is able to cite a statutory case from the Jewish legal tradition which supports it. He functions as a judge, not as a moral authority. Indeed, without suh a prooftext, it is interesting to speculate on whether he would have, or could have, raised the issue at all. Moreover, the haste with which Kluger provides other textual arguments of a non-moral nature, and the thoroughness with which he discusses them, may well imply to the reader that the moral considerations advanced by Kluger are ultimately *"divre musar,"* words of ethical sensitivity, which, while important, possess, in the end, a secondary status.

The issue is an important one because it touches upon the larger question of the relationship between law and morality in Judaism. No scholar of Jewish law would dispute the above-cited statements of Elon and Spero about the appearance of the "moral imperative" in many Jewish legal matters. Certainly, the passage from *Megillah* and Kluger's appropriation of its sentiments in his responsum testify to the fact that this imperative frequently operates within Jewish law and that, at times, it is "actionable." As Aharon Lichtenstein, in his piece, "Does Jewish Tradition Recognize an Ethic Independent of Halakha?," puts it, "the ethical moment" in Judaism is "in its own way fully imperative."[25] Eugene Borowitz, commenting upon this statement, observes the following:

> The critical yet easily overlooked part of this statement is the qualifying clause, "in its own way." That is, Lichtenstein does not say: "and commitment to an ethical moment that though different from Halakha is nevertheless of a piece with it and fully imperative." No, the "ethical moment" . . . is "fully imperative" only "in its own way." Just what is that distinctive way? And what are its implications?[26]

Borowitz, by posing these questions to Lichtenstein, causes the reader to wonder whether Schwarzschild's claim—that Jewish law offers "a judgment procedure which makes sure that the application of the law *in each individual case* is proper (i.e., moral) "—is phenomenologically correct. For as Borowitz points out, Lichtenstein himself makes plain the fact that rabbis throughout history have not operationalized ethical values in issuing all their decisions. At times, it is true, these values are of prime import for a rabbinic authority in deciding a case. On other occasions, however, they are either ignored or overruled.[27] In this way, Lichtenstein's scholarship and Borowitz's interpretations sensitize the student of the responsa to the fact "that though the ethical impulse is there" in Jewish law, "it has," or may have, "much less imperative status than the *din* (a law). . . . Moreover, it only gains 'the full force of obligation . . . once it has been determined' that an ethical issue is involved. This determination is not a matter left to the general conscience, but is assigned to competent decisors and permitted to function by them only in a limited number of cases."[28] In sum, Borowitz feels that when there is a tension in Jewish law between the demands of morality and the imperative of the law, it is the "legal" and not the "moral" imperative which is authoritative. As Borowitz concludes, "The ethical must make a case for itself should there be a conflict between them (the legal and the ethical). Even then its legitimacy and functioning will be defined by legists."[29]

The onus, then, in a case such as the one in the Kluger responsum, *is* upon Kluger, and not Nathanson, to demonstrate the legal relevance and, therefore, the imperative nature of the moral concern.

Since the "legitimacy and functioning" of this concern is, in the end, defended through legal categories, it may, as we have seen in the case of Nathanson, be rejected altogether. Ethical values, *as independent standards*, apparently do not have a *prima facie* claim to authority within Jewish law. Of course, as Borowitz observes, "All this is not astonishing for a legal system. Rather, an open-minded student would probably show great admiration for the Jewish community in creating a legal structure which is so highly ethical. (However), the ethical, which ought to come (from a Liberal perspective) as a categorical or unmediated imperative," may well operate "within Judaism," at times, as a "subsidiary consideration."[30] The point of this discussion is not to resolve the debate over the exact nature of the relationship between law and morality in Judaism. Indeed, the evidence of the Kluger responsum and the mention of Nathanson's response to it hardly provide enough material to even attempt such a resolution. Rather, the purpose of these considerations is to sensitize the reader to this issue and to indicate that it is a subject for continued debate and interest.

Afterword

In examining the Kluger responsum from several perspectives, it has been the aim of this paper to present the richness of one aspect of the Jewish legal tradition to the reader. The complexity of the responsa literature, and the numerous angles of investigation it demands, bespeaks both the ongoing vitality of the process of Jewish legal hermeneutics and the need for continued research in this all too often neglected field. This essay, through its analysis and exposition of the Kluger responsum, has hopefully stimulated further inquiry into the nature and processes of the legal tradition within Judaism.

TRANSLATION OF THE TEXT

A responsum of His Excellence of Excellencies, Paragon of the Generation, the Chief Shepherd, the One Who Gives Joy to All the Earth, the Light of Israel, and its Holiness, its Chariot and Horsemen (II Kings 2:12), May his light shine, Servant of the Lord, Glory of the Sages, Rabbi of all the Children of the Exile, His Holy and Glorious Name, Our Teacher and Rabbi, Rabbi Solomon Kluger, May his light shine, Head of the Exile and Head of the Yeshiva in the Distinguished Holy Community of Brody, May the Lord found it well.

With the help of God, Monday of the Weekly Torah Portion "And these are the statutes which you shall place before them," in the year 5718, (1857–1858) in Brody.

Great peace and blessing from the One Who dwells in the Heavens to His Honor, my Friend, the Rabbi, the Great Light, Learned and Sharpwitted, the Perfect Sage, the Crown of Torah, Our Teacher, Rabbi Hayyim Nathan, May his Light shine, Who Sits on the Seat of Justice in the Holy Community of Cracow, May the Lord found it well; and especially to my friend, the Eminent Rabbi, (Scion) of the Prominent Family, the Famous Lord, Prince of the Congregation, Crown of Torah, Our Teacher, Rabbi Lebush Halevi Horowitz, May his light shine, Redeemer and Rescuer of the Holy Community of Cracow, May it be founded well.

Behold, I received your letter today, Sunday, towards evening, and although I was troubled and weary, I resolved to answer you immediately tonight, for the matter is pressing, as the days of Passover, with the help of God, are imminent. And in an enormously large city [like Cracow] it is necessary to begin to ask and to investigate [at least] thirty days before Passover. Now, concerning your question as to whether [it is permissible] to bake *matzot* for Passover with the [type of] machine that has been introduced into the German states; behold, that which was told you, that we do so here in our community, is a total lie, completely unfounded. Indeed, it would not occur to anyone to do this for several reasons, which I will clarify [below]. Furthermore, one does not learn from the Germans for several reasons.

Behold, the reason for the prohibition against this appears first and foremost to be that it is not within the framework *(geder)* of the upright and the moral to plunder the poor who are anxiously awaiting [the performance of] this [commandment]. For from the assistance they provide [in the baking of] *matzot,* they have a significant source of income *(sa'ad gadol)* for the many Passover expenses which accrue to our people. Thus, it is stated in the first chapter of *Megillah* (*Babylonian Talmud, Megillah* 4b), "But at any rate, all agree that the *Megillah* (Scroll of Esther) is not be read on the Sabbath. . . . Rabbi Joseph said, "It is because the poor are anxiously awaiting the reading of the *Megillah*.'" Refer to the *Tosafot* (medieval rabbinic commentators upon the Talmud), who commented on this Talmudic passage, "that even in a place where there is no fear that [the prohibition], 'Lest one carry it,'"[31] be violated, it is still forbidden [to read the *Megillah* on the Sabbath] for the reason cited above. For while the reading of the *Megillah* is an obligation, the words of the Oral Tradition *(divrei kabbalah)* cancelled it on account of the poor who anxiously await the reading of the *Megillah*. All the more so, then, with this [practice], where there is no custom [to perform] this commandment with a machine. Therefore, one should not do this, as the poor anxiously await this [task] in order to earn wages for Passover.

In addition, several middle-class householders and, all the more so, common people, do not contribute *Me'ot Ḥitin*[32]—as is customary among [the people] Israel, and the source of which [is derived] from the words of the early medieval rabbinic authorities *(rishonim)*, may their memory be for a blessing. Therefore, [by employing the poor in the baking of *matzot*], they thereby fulfill somewhat [the practice of *Me'ot Hitin*], for at least they give the poor the opportunity to earn wages [for the purchase of Passover necessities] through their help [in the performance of] the commandments. Yet, it will not be so if they also stop [the poor from assisting in the baking of *matzot*], as they have [already] neglected the commandment of charity and the practice of *Me'otHitin* for Passover.

Aside from this, it seems to me that there are three reasons why this is forbidden according to the Law. One is that it certainly is not permissible to fulfill one's obligation concerning the consumption of *matzah* on Passover[33] through those produced by a machine. This is because the Law has established for us [the ruling] that one is not exempt from fulfilling this commandment if a deaf-mute, an idiot, or a child produces it, as none of them are regarded as mentally competent. Moreover, even if an adult Jew stands beside one of them [in order to supervise their baking, the *matzah*] still cannot be produced by one of them. And if this is so, certainly the workings of this machine are not to be preferred to the labor of a minor who possesses no mature reasoning faculty, nor from the others, even if a mature adult stands by [and oversees their work]. For it has been the intention of rabbinic authorities [throughout the centuries to see to it] that the *matzah* of commandment *(matzat mitzvah)* requires careful supervision by an adult Jew from the first moment [the flour] is kneaded until the process is completed in the final moment of its baking. As this is so concerning the *matzah* of commandment, clearly (Jews) are not exempt [from fulfilling the commandment with machine-baked *matzah*]. Moreover, the majority of our people, who are unable to draw a distinction between most *matzah* and that of *mitzvah*, will consume machine-baked *matzah* as *matzat mitzvah* and will not fulfill the commandment through the eating of genuine *matzat mitzvah*. Thus, they will recite a blessing in vain. Therefore, it is fitting to decree—inasmuch as *matzat mitzvah* is a decree from the Torah—that one does not fulfill one's obligation concerning the commandment of *matzat mitzvah* with this machine-baked *matzah*. Also, from this it would follow that if one forgot and did not eat the *afikomen* as legislated in the *Shulchan Aruch*[34]—where it states that if one did not eat *matzat mitzvah* which has been supervised from the moment of reaping there is no need to return and eat, as one can rely upon the *matzah* one has eaten during the festive meal—, and as our "regular" *matzah* is called "*matzah*," *since the worker (haozer)* knows that he is producing *matzah* which is to be likened to those of *mitzvah*, for in his view all of them are for *mitzvah;* however, it would not be so if they were produced by a machine, as one would certainly not thereby be exempt from the *mitzvah* of *matzah* and a sin would thereby come from this. This is the first reason.

Secondly, it is stated in the second chapter of *Pesachim* (*Babylonian Talmud, Pesachim* 36b), "And they all agree that dough may not be kneaded with lukewarm water." And the Talmud raises an objection there, as it is written, "Why is it different from meal-offerings, as it is taught in the Mishnah, 'All meal-offerings are kneaded with lukewarm water and the official in charge guards them so that they will not become leaven'"? And they rebut, "If this was said of very careful men (priests), shall it also be said of men who are not so careful"? Behold, it is proven from this that it would be permissible [to knead the dough] in lukewarm water as it is possible that it would not leaven. Rather, it is only because it requires supervision that it is forbidden [to knead the dough] in lukewarm water. This implies that "regular" *matzah* does not require such careful supervision since those who work the dough do so with their hands; and the entire time that the workers do so the *matzah* dough will not ferment by itself. Moreover, there is no reason to suspect that the worker will overheat the *matzah* dough later without actual effort, as why should he do this? However, when it required both strict attention and supervision, we are not free to depend upon it. And if this is so, certainly one must insist upon strict attention and supervision with *matzah* baked by a machine. For first, who knows, if a machine breaks, [that the dough] will not leaven? We find nothing concerning this [in the legal rulings] of the rabbis. Instead, only the work of a man with his hands [is discussed], as this has more validity. And who is able to control nature? For even if one insures that it will not leaven [during the kneading], since the machine first kneads [the dough] and then, by necessity, forms circular *matzot* through a round mold [presumably the *matzah* could leaven during the midst of this procedure as there would be a lag between operations]. Aside from this, many crumbs and pieces of dough remain stuck in the machine. Thus, it is certainly forbidden to include these extra bits in a later batch by mixing them in with the rest of the dough, as those bits which remain even a short time after the preparation leaven immediately. Since this is so, it is necessary to burn the crumbs from the machine in order to be certain that they will not be mixed in with the dough as well as to insure that these extra bits will not sometime later be mixed in with other dough. And behold, all this requires extra supervision. Certainly, *matzah* baked by a machine is no better than kneading in lukewarm water, for even though this might be considered possible with [proper] supervision, it is forbidden. In addition, we know that frequently whole or broken wheat [which is more likely to leaven and is, therefore, forbidden], will be found in the *matzot*. For time testifies that God has granted me the merit of serving as a rabbi in various cities for fifty years, and not one year has passed in which questions such as these have not arisen. Thus, these issues arise when the worker, utilizing his hand, feels something and asks a question. However, if a machine is used, who will feel if there is a [piece] of wheat or a portion of it in the *matzah*? How can we rely upon someone checking upon this later? Rather, we fear it will be overlooked. And as we are not among the "meticulous men" mentioned in the Talmudic passage (*Pesachim* 36b) cited above, one does not rely upon us for a matter that requires strict supervision.

And there is a third reason, as cited in the second chapter of *Pesachim* 37a, concerning the statement that one must not make Syrian cakes (pita bread) shaped in figures on Passover. "And Boethus ben Zonin objected, 'It is possible to make it in a mold which would form it without delay.'" And they taught, "Then shall it be said, all Syrian cakes shaped in figures are forbidden, but the Syrian cakes of Boethus are permitted"!? Behold, in this matter, there is a dispute among the rabbinic authorities. However, the Law, as established in the Tur, Shulchan Aruch,[35] states "All Syrian cakes are forbidden, whether those of bakers or of private persons." As this is so, then this is the authentic law of the Talmud. And if, in this case where all the work is done by a Jew, and only the shape was in a mold, it is still forbidden—as it is said, "All Syrian cakes shaped in figures are forbidden, but the Syrian cakes of Boethus are permitted"!?— then all the more so if all the work will be done in a mold. Thus, it is proper to say that all *matzot* which are not made by an adult (Jewish) man are forbidden, and God forbid that one should assert that those made by a machine are permissible for use.

Therefore, do not veer from the custom of your fathers. The Germans will do as their heart desires, as is their way. However, we will walk in the footsteps of our fathers and will depart from them neither to the right nor to the left. May their merit protect us and cause us to return quickly to the land of our fathers in our own day.

Your friend, troubled in soul and weak in strength, (begs your) leave. The Young One,

Solomon Kluger

NOTES

[1] The author would like to express his thanks to his friend, Michael Rosen, and his colleagues, Michael Signer and William Cutter and Steven Passamaneck, for having read and discussed various parts of this essay with him.

[2] See the *Jerusalem Talmud, Peah* 17a, where it states, "Even that which a veteran pupil will one day recite before his master was already revealed to Moses at Sinai."

[3] For a consideration of the impact social reality has upon the responsa literature, see Solomon Freehof, *The Responsa Literature* (New York, 1973), pp. 42–43.

[4] A full consideration of the bitter rabbinic debate which has continued over this matter through the first half of the twentieth century can be found in *Ibid.*, pp. 181–189.

[5] *Ibid.*, p. 183.

6 See Isadore Twersky, *Introduction to the Code of Maimonides* (New Haven and London, 1980), pp. 92–93.

7 This concept is taken from Max Kadushin, *The Rabbinic Mind* (New York, 1952).

8 The use and structure of the epistle as a medieval legal document is thoroughly and brilliantly discussed in Leonard Boyle, "Diplomatics," James M. Powell, ed., *Medieval Studies* (Syracuse, New York, 1976), pp. 69–101. I am indebted to my colleague Michael Signer for bringing this source to my attention.

9 Robert Kirschner discusses the form and structure of the classical responsum in his introduction to his forthcoming book, *Rabbinic Responsa of the Holocaust Era*. I am grateful to him for sharing his manuscript with me.

10 David A.J. Richards, *The Moral Criticism of the Law* (Encino and Belmont, CA., 1977), p. 26.

11 *Ibid.*, p. 28.

12 This quotation is taken from the Soncino English translation of the *Babylonian Talmud, Megillah*, p. 19, ft. 3.

13 For a summary of Nathanson's position, see Freehof, *The Responsa Literature*, pp. 184–185.

14 Lawrence A. Hoffman, *The Canonization of the Synagogue Service* (Notre Dame and London, 1979), p. 15.

15 Mordecai Hacohen, "Solomon Kluger," *Encyclopedia Judaica* (Jerusalem, 1971), Volume 10, columns 1110–1111.

16 Kluger's responsum is reported in Louis Jacobs, *Theology in the Responsa* (London and Boston, 1975), p. 285.

17 *Ibid.*, p. 286.

18 On the transformations that altered the nature of Jewish life in this era, see Jacob Katz, *Out of the Ghetto* (Cambridge, 1973).

19 Peter Berger uses these terms in his article, "A Sociological View of the Secularization of Theology," *Journal for the Scientific Study of Religion* 6:1 (1967), p. 12.

20 Ismar Schorsch, *Jewish Reactions to German Anti-Semitism, 1870–1914* (New York and Philadelphia, 1972), p. 10.

21 Richards, *The Moral Criticism of the Law*, p. 30.

22 Steven S. Schwarzschild, "The Question of Jewish Ethics Today," *Sh'ma* 7/124, p. 31.

23 Elon is quoted by Shubert Spero in Spero's *Morality, Halakha, and Jewish Tradition* (New York, 1983), p. 184.

24 *Ibid.*

25 Quoted in Eugene Borowitz, "The Authority of the Ethical Impulse in Halakha," in Jonathan V. Plaut, ed., *Through the Sound of Many Voices: Writings Contributed on the Occasion of the 70th Birthday of W. Gunther Plaut* (Toronto, 1982), p. 163.

26 *Ibid.*, p. 159.

27 *Ibid.*, pp. 159–164. See especially p. 162, where it is written, "Most Jewish authorities do not consider the need to act in this ethical fashion a *din* (law)." Moreover, David Weiss Halivni, in an interesting article, entitled 'Can a Religious Law be Immoral?,' in Arthur A. Chiel, ed., *Perspectives on Jews and Judaism: Essays in honor of Wolfe Kelman*, p. 165, states, 'The notion that the Rabbis of the Talmud were aware of a possible conflict between morality and religious law, and consciously resolved in favor of morality, cannot be defended historically.' Weiss Halivni's scholarship thus stands in opposition to the positions advanced by Schwartzchild, Spero, and Elon cited above.

28 *Ibid.*, p. 163.

29 *Ibid.*, p. 166.

30 *Ibid.*

31 Carrying from the private to the public domain on the Sabbath is forbidden on the

basis of *Exodus* 16:29, "Abide ye every man in his place, let no man go out of his place on the seventh day"; and *Jeremiah* 17:21–22, "Thus saith the Lord, 'Take heed for the sake of your souls, and bear no burden on the sabbath day, . . . neither carry forth a burden out of your houses on the sabbath day . . .'" As a result, one reason given for the prohibition of the reading of the *Megillah* on Saturday was that rabbinic authorities wanted to prevent individuals from inadvertently carrying the Scroll of Esther from their homes (a private domain) to the synagogue (which would involve carrying into a public domain).

[32] In Talmudic times this term referred to a collection made before Passover to ensure a supply of flour for *matzot* for the poor. By the Middle Ages this custom was codified in the *Shulchan Aruch, Orach Hayyim* 429:1 and, in modern times, the custom has been broadened to include all the holiday needs of the poor at Passover.

[33] The positive duty of eating a quantity of *matzah* equivalent to at least the size of an olive applies only to the first night (two nights in the Diaspora) of the holiday. The source for this custom is found in *Exodus* 12:18, "In the first month, on the fourteenth day of the month at evening, you shall eat unleavened bread. . . ."

[34] The *afikomen* refers to the middle *matzah* on the Passover *seder* plate. This *matzah* is broken into two pieces by the leader of the *seder*, and the larger portion is referred to as the afikomen. A symbolic reminder of the paschal sacrifice, it is not eaten until the very end of the meal. The legislation referred to in the Kluger responsum is found in the Shulchan Aruch, *Orach Hayyim* 277:2.

[35] This law is found in *Tur, Shulchan Aruch* 460.

RESPONSE TO DAVID ELLENSON
A LIVING TRADITION: ONGOING JEWISH EXEGESIS

Elliot N. Dorff
Univeristy of Judaism, Los Angeles

A. *The Status of the Bible in Jewish Legal Development*

Christian readers are probably somewhat perplexed after reading Dr. Ellenson's article by the proliferation of sources which he cites. What happened to the Bible in all of this? And how is any of this the word of God?

The problem at its core is a familiar one in the history of both Christianity and Judaism. Paul wanted to replace observance of the Law with adherence to the Spirit,[1] but even he had to spell out the demands of the Spirit in rather legalistic terms when it became clear that the Galatians had no idea of what he meant by living by the Spirit.[2] The later Roman Catholic Church carried this further by developing a body of canon law every bit as complex as Jewish law. The Protestant Reformation was, in part, a reaction to this and an attempt to get back to living by the Spirit, and Protestant sects to this day talk about living by Scripture. At the same time, however, they have developed their own interpretations of what living by the Bible means, and that often entails specific requirements and prohibitions. In some cases Protestants have established rules governing virtually all of life, including the clothes one wears, the books one reads, the food one eats, and the people with whom one socializes—to say nothing of more distinctly "religious" things like the service one gives to the community and the activities from which one refrains on the Sabbath. Puritans, Mormons, Amish, and Seventh Day Adventists come readily to mind, but the same is also true for most other Protestant sects in one degree or another.

My point is not to call into question the seriousness of the Christian claim to live by the Word instead of the Law. It is rather to indicate that anyone who wants to live by the Word—Christian, Jew, or Muslim—

must first *interpret* and *apply* it. for sometimes the Biblical text is ambiguous, and sometimes it does not speak about a given situation at all. Even when its meaning is clear, its application to present circumstances may not be. To take a Christian example, should Paul's pronouncements about the status of women[3] be understood as the inviolable Word of God, or are they merely a reflection of proper conduct as understood in his society with no Biblical authority for ours? Living by the Bible is clearly not as simple as it first seems; interpretation is required.

But as soon as one admits human interpretation, the divine authority of the results is at risk. For even if the interpreter links the interpretation directly to a Biblical text, who is to say that an alternative explanation is not preferable? Canons of interpretation have been developed, but they rarely preclude an interpretation or enable even an outside observer to judge between alternatives because they generally do not give sufficient guidance in the all-important task of *weighing* the options. Matters get even worse when reasonably plausible interpretations of two Biblical passages produce diametrically opposite results—not, unfortunately, an uncommon occurrence. Whenever there is even the slightest disagreement about the meaning of a verse, human beings inevitably must decide what it mens, and then one must wonder whether it is the word of God that one is hearing or the word of a human being.

The Jewish tradition faced these issues head-on. It claimed that revelation in the form of direct comunication with God had ceased after the destruction of the First Temple in 586 B.C.E. Even before that time, the revelation to Moses (i.e., the Five Books of Moses known as the "Torah") was superior to all other revelations because the other Prophets "looked through nine lenses whereas Moses looked only through one; they looked through a cloudy lens while Moses looked through one that was clear."[4] Consequently, after the First Temple period God's word was to be communicated through interpretation of the original, authoritative revelation contained in the Torah.

> Rabbi Abdimi from Haifa said: Since the day when the Temple was destroyed, the prophetic gift was taken away from the prophets and given to the Sages.—Is then a Sage not a Prophet?—What he meant was this: although it has been taken from the prophets, it has not been taken from the Sages. Amemar said: A Sage is even superior to a prophet, as it says, "And a prophet has a heart of wisdom" (Psalms 90:12). Who is (usually) compared with whom? Is not the smaller compared with the greater?[5]

This, of course, opens the door to a variety of different readings, and, indeed a characteristic of Judaism is the lively debate it fostered in the proper interpretation of its sources. The price that one pays for that is consistency and coherence: a multitude of interpretations inevitably means that some disagree with each other, at least in emphasis, and that ultimately challenges the integrity of the tradition and its ability to speak in one voice. But the Rabbis were willing to tolerate problems in those areas because they believed that the various, ongoing interpretations were all the authoritative words of God.

> Lest a man say, "Since some scholars declare a thing impure and others declare it pure, some pronounce a thing forbidden and others permitted, some disqualify an object while others uphold its fitness, how can I study Torah under such cirumstances"? Scripture says, "They are given from one shepherd" (Eccles. 12:11): One God has given them, one leader (Moses) has uttered them at the command of the Lord of all creation, blessed be He, as it says, "And God spoke *all* these words" (Ex. 20:1). You on your part must then make your ear like a grain receiver and acquire a heart that can understand the words of the scholars who declare a thing impure as well as those who declare it pure, the words of those who declare a thing forbidden as well as those who pronounce it permitted, and the words of those who disqualify an object as well as those who uphold its fitness. . . . Although one scholar offers his view and another offers his, the words of both are all derived from what Moses, the shepherd, received from the One Lord of the Universe.[6]

It is for this reason that so many texts of interpretation are developed in Judaism and that the Bible is rarely quoted directly. As the Rabbis put it,

> "For your beloved ones are better than wine" (Song of Songs 1:2). This means that the words of the beloved ones (the Sages) are better than the wine of Torah. Why? Because one cannot give a proper decision from the words of the Torah since the Torah is ambiguous and consists entirely of headings. . . . From the words of the Sages, however, one can derive the proper law because they explain the Torah.[7]

In this Jewish law is similar to American law. Legal briefs rarely cite the Constitution; they rely instead on the most recent precedents relevant to the case. That, of couse, does *not* mean that the Constitution becomes irrelevant to American law. It continues to function as the foundation of the law, giving it its fundamental principles and mode of operation. Similarly, in Jewish law the Bible continues to be studied and understood as the basic norm that provides its essential standards, methodology, and authority.

In other words, what Dr. Ellenson says about the Talmud is true of the Torah too. The Biblical "statutory" text is theoretically more authoritative than the later, "precedential" discussions and decisions, but in reality the later sources define the meaning of the Bible for the Jewish tradition. That might well be different from the meaning of the Bible as understood in Christian, Muslim, or secular circles, and that is why Judaism is very much the religion of the Bible *as interpreted by the Rabbis,* just as Christianity is the religion of the Bible as interpreted by the Church Fathers and their successors. And just as it would be misleading to assert that the Talmud is cast aside when the responsum cites the *Tur* for its authority, so it would be misleading to claim that the Bible is ignored when its later interpretations are used and not the Bible itself. None of the three Western religions relies on the Bible alone, but none of them is totally independent of it either. In each the Bible functions as the foundation of the principles, methodology, and authority of the later tradition. And, of course, each claims that *its* understanding and expansion of the Bible carries the authority of God.[8]

B. *How a Text Means*

Dr. Ellenson artfully points out the interlocking textual, social, psychological, and moral factors which go into formulating a responsum. The way in which legal precedents are read depends upon the situation of the reader as well as the precedents themselves.

There are several points here which I would like to underscore. First, the contextual factors which influence the decisor *do not* form a base of authority independent of the texts; if anything, the reverse is true. The Bible, Talmud, codes, and responsa constitute a body of sacred literature whose imperatives can be ignored as little as God can be. Moreover, from a positivistic, legal point of view, those texts are both definitional and legally operational: any rabbi who intends to issue a decision *in Jewish law* must link his decision to that corpus of literature, for it both defines the decision as a part of the ongoing tradition of Jewish interpretation and gives it authority within the Jewish community. The parallels to American law are obvious here: no matter how much a court wants to deviate from the substance of previous decisions, it must somehow link its decision to the precedents, however tenuously. In most cases the linkage will be strong and logically cogent; that what gives any legal system continuity and coherence. Consequently, as Dr. Ellenson says, the law can attain a "semi-autonomous" state in which decisions are made without reference to anything but legal precedents. On the other hand, contextual factors can never replace the mooring of a decision in the legal sources.

If relativists are blind to the necessity of connecting a decision to the previous literature, absolutists and literalists are equally blind to the interaction of the law with the society for which it is intended. Dr. Ellenson points out the operation of contextual factors in the formulation of this responsum, and I would stress that the same is true for the Talmud and, indeed, for the Bible itself. The import of applying historical methods to the study of the Bible is precisely that one recognizes that cultural factors influenced both its mode of expression and its content. That is why traditionalists object so strongly to such analysis: it becomes hard to discern in the Bible where the human hand stops and the divine hand begins. Then one questions the authority of the whole document. That is a hard problem, but modernists struggle with it because they know that, like it or not, they must confront the truth that the Bible was written for a given historical society with its needs and customs in mind. As a result, the Bible and Talmud, as well as the responsa, must be understood against the background in which they were created.

But then the genetic fallacy must be avoided: the original meaning of a text is not necessarily its most important meaning. Ongoing traditions of interpretation impart new, and often more interesting, meanings to the text as people in later generations see new things in it and apply it to new contexts. That is why the Bible is not the end of the matter but is rather the source of living traditions.

All of the above considerations are true not only of legal texts like responsa; they apply equally to all genres of literature. On the one hand, the original text and all subsequent texts that interpret it occupy an ontological realm independent of ours and have an integrity all their own. On the other, their original and later meanings can only be discerned if one is aware of the contexts in which they were written and read. For those serious about reading the Bible, both points must be embraced and balanced.

C. *Law and Morality within Judaism*

Christians are used to thinking of Jewish law in the way in which the New Testament describes it. For Paul the law is spiritually and morally dangerous, and the path to salvation is therefore not through law but rather through being born again into faith. The Pharisees are portrayed as nasty, legalistic people who lack compassion and moral concern.

Jews have never seen it that way. They rather have resonated with the words of the Psalmist:

> The law of the Lord is perfect, renewing life;
>   the decrees of the Lord are enduring,
>   making the simple wise.
> The precepts of the Lord are just,
>   rejoicing the heart;
>   the commandment of the Lord shines clear,
>   making the eyes light up.

> I have hurried and not delayed
> to keep your commandments . . .
> I arise at midnight to praise You
> for Your just rules.
> I am a companion to all who fear You,
> to those who keep Your precepts.
> Your steadfast love, O Lord, fills the earth;
> teach me Your laws.[9]

In sharp contrast to Christianity, for Judaism the law is the most explicit expression of morality and the primary educational tool to inculcate moral knowledge, intention, and action. Jewish sources recognize a realm of morality beyond the law, and they demand that Jews follow moral rules; but they also assert that the law is itself the most trustworthy and adequate articulation of what it means to be moral.[10]

Because Jewish law so thoroughly assumes that the law is moral there is one section of Dr. Ellenson's paper that I would question. He points out that in Kluger's responsum, "The ethical imperative, the realization of the 'upright and the moral,' plays a determinative role." In contrast, "Ethical postures, in Nathanson's view, simply have no bearing in the case." Is it that, or is it that Nathanson simply thinks that the Jewish moral and legal concern for the impoverished bakers can be met in other ways? I doubt that Rabbi Nathanson was any less moral than Rabbi Kluger; it simply was Nathanson's judgment that care of the poor, which Judaism unreservedly demands, could be accomplished without prohibiting machine-baked *matzot*. The issue is not whether ethics is relevant to a legal decision in Jewish law; it always is. The issue is rather whether the moral concern which the two rabbis share should be met in this way or some other.

Aside from the question of the existence and authority of a realm of morals separate from the law, Jewish philosophers debate another question: to what extent does morality play a role in the very formulation of the law? Some Orthodox and Reform theorists deny that it plays any role at all. From that they draw opposite conclusions. The Orthodox, taking a literalist approach, say that only those moral concerns which are already encased in law can be the basis of any future decisions; morality on its own has no independent authority. The Reform use this denial to claim that the law should have no authority at all; only morality should be our guide. Conservative ideologues maintain that moral concerns have always influenced the rabbis charged with shaping the law, and they should continue to do so.[11]

However that issue is resolved, the pervasive concern for morality in the sources of Jewish law insures that it will continue to be the fount of moral wisdom and instruction that the Psalmist appreciated.

NOTES

[1] *Romans*, Chs. 7–9; *Galatians*, Chs. 2–3.
[2] *Galatians* 5; cf. also *Romans* 13–15.
[3] *I Corinthians* 11:1–16.
[4] *Leviticus Rabbah* 1:14.
[5] *Bava Batra* 12a.
[6] *Numbers Rabbah* 14:4; cf. also *Eruvin* 13b.
[7] *Ibid.*

[8] For further discussion and sources on the points of this section, cf. my article, "Judaism as a Religious Legal System," *Hastings Law Journal*, 29:6 (July, 1978), 1331–1360.

[9] *Psalms* 19:8–9; 119:60, 62–64.

[10] Cf. my article, "The Interaction of Jewish Law with Morality," *Judaism*, 26:4 (Fall, 1977), 455–466 for a presentation and discussion of some of the primary sources on this.

[11] In addition to the sources cited in notes 21–24 of Ellenson's article, cf., among others, Marvin Fox, *Modern Jewish Ethics* (Columbus, Ohio: Ohio State University Press, 1975); Seymour Siegel, *Conservative Judaism and Jewish Law* (New York: KTAV, 1977), pp. 123–132.

RESPONSE TO DAVID ELLENSON
LAW, ETHICS AND RITUAL IN JEWISH DECISION MAKING

Daniel Landes
Yeshiva University of Los Angeles

The relation of law *(Halakha)* to ethics and ritual in Judaism has long bedeviled precise formulation. To this potent mix has been added, recently, the influence of the social-historical context upon sacred and legal text exegesis. These four factors are interwoven within Rabbi Kluger's responsum. In David Ellenson's lucid exposition the ritual is the baking of the *matza*. Halakha governs the requirements of that procedure, ethics is the concern for the poor potentially disenfranchised by the machine process of baking, and the social-historical context is the perceived disintegrating impact of Western modernity upon Jewish religious life.

Dr. Ellenson carefully unravels the strands of the responsum and concludes that while the *Halakha* possesses an "integrity of its own" how it is to be interpreted bespeaks, to a high degree, a motivation properly found in the social-historical context of the period and within the personality and psychology of the decisor. It is there where a "deeper, more complex understanding of the Jewish legal process (to) [may] emerge." Following Eugene Borowitz he recognizes the existence of "moral considerations" in Halakha but sees it, and this responsum is one example, to be "utimately *divre musar*, words of ethical sensitivity, which, while important, possess, in the end, a secondary status."

Underlying this argument is an assumption that the traditional process of Jewish decision making is based upon a formalistic *Halakha*. Texts function as a set of rules of law in a highly structured and basically static system which is paradoxically (or perhaps due to this formal objectivity) actually prey to very subjective interpretation. On this basis, Dr. Ellenson separates *Halakha,* and for that matter ritual, from ethics and religious feeling. I believe, however, that beneath the placid looking waters of the surface codified *Halakha* are powerful and turbulent currents. They exert a great pull upon the "elitist" swimmers in "the sea of the Talmud," and must be plumbed by later analysts in order to discover motivation in decision-making and the complex and dialectical relation between law and ethics and between those two and ritual.

To understand the motivation underlying the second and the apparently more technical half of the responsum one must ascertain the relation between *Hametz* (leaven) and *Matzah* (unleavened bread) and the nature of ritual supervision that the latter demands. *Hametz* and *Matzah* are reciprocally defined categories.

The *Mekhilta* explicates:

> Seven Days Thou Shalt Eat Unleavened Bread (Ex. XII: 15). I might understand this to mean unleavened bread of any kind; therefore it says: 'Thou shalt eat no leavened bread with it' (Deut. XVI: 3). The Law, then, applies only to such kinds as could be leavened as well as unleavened. And which are those? They are the five species, namely: wheat, barley, spelt, oats, and rye. Rice, millet, poppyseed, sesame and legumes, which cannot be leavened as well as unleavened, but which decay, are thus excluded.[1]
>
> *And there shall No Leavened Bread Be Seen With Thee*, etc. (Deut. XVI: 4). This compares leaven to leavened bread and leavened bread to leaven . . . just as the one, leavened bread is forbidden only when it is made of one of the five species, so also is the other, leaven, forbidden only when it comes from one of the five species.[2]

The preparation of *Matzot* (plural) therefore is a risky and potentially dangerous ritual undertaking. One must use grain which could become *hametz* in the very process of kneading or baking. Worse still, the grain itself if subjected to water prior to the baking process might undergo undetected leavening. It is not surprising that the storage of grain and the preparation of Matzah is customarily prohibited on Passover itself.[3] Preventing the *Matzot* from becoming *hametz* falls under [the precept of eating] unleavened bread."[4] The two types of guarding guarding of the preparation of the *Matzot* so that no leavening occurs. The Talmud, however, understands this to be a guarding "for the sake of [the precept of eating] unleavened bread."[103] The two types of guarding function together as Rashi (1040–1105) explains "intend all guarding from *Hametz* [of Matzah] as being prepared to serve as commanded *Matzah* [eaten on Passover night of first day]."[5] For the nonobligatory *Matzah* of "filing one's belly" only the "guarding from *Hametz*" is needed.[6] While distinct the conscious guarding of intent [to serve as the commanded *matzah*] "always requires the practical "guarding from *Hametz*" as its content of action.[7]

Both guardings exhibit in their *Halakhic* development a wide degree of elasticity. Guarding from *Hametz* is at its basis an assessment of fact—that this bread in preparation is and remains unleavened. On this basis Rav Huna, in an accepted statement in the Talmud, claims that even the kneaded dough of a Gentile can be considered perfectly fit to be consumed on Passover-presumably if one can ascertain *(makir)* by a sight test that it is *hametz* free.[8] Later authorities, however, required an actual guarding by a commanded individual fully sensitive to and bound by the prohibition of *Hametz*.[9] This activist approach contributes a profound conservation to the *Matzah* preparation—everything possible must be done to prevent absolutely any leavening from occurring. At the same time activism exists in tension with the conservative desire. Thus the Talmudic Sage Raba, as interpreted by Ramban (1194–1270), considered the controversial practice of washing the grain prior to its grinding, hereby producing a finer flour to be obligatory. He actually desired the danger of leavening to be increased in order to necessitate a more sophisticated and active guarding.[10] But the conservative tendency prevailed. Not only was Raba's bold requirement denied as obligatory in the Talmud but in succeeding generations the *Geonim* (589–1038) in an act of religious reticence went so far as to forbid the practice and to eliminate with it a possible avenue of leavening.[11]

What is the source of this almost obsessive expansion of guarding from *hametz* which as its base was only an assessment of fact? Paul Ricoeur offers a suggestive interpretation of the rabbinic propensity for increase observance: The scrupulous conscience is an increasingly articulated and subtle conscience that forgets nothing and adds incessantly to its obligations; it is a manifold and sedimented conscience that finds salvation only in a movement; it accumulates behind itself an enormous past that makes tradition; it is alive only at its point, at the forward end of tradition, where it "interprets," in new circumstances, equivocations or contradictions. This is not a conscience that begins or begins anew, but a conscience that continues and adds to. If its work of minute and often minuscule innovation stops, the conscience is caught in the trip of its own tradition, which becomes its yoke.[12]

Ricoeur's bluntly worded, judgmental but useful analysis needs to be balanced by the parallel expansion of increased religious devotion through further development of guarding of intent. The Talmud itself minimally mandates a guarding of this type during the kneading process.[13] This guarding[14] was extended by many back to the time of grinding and even by others to the harvest itself.[15] It was extended forward to include the baking itself.[16]

The double guarding was domesticated into a generally moderate and reduced formula in the codified *Halakha* that Rabbi Kluger appeals to.[17] Nevertheless the more radical potentialities still exist latent within the exposited texts. As Judaism is a learning centered tradition this presents an ever renewed encounter with these options of observance. And these options lose their theoretical nature when they become actualized possibilities in the supererogatory gesture.[18] In fact, some practices in this manifestation have greatly exceeded the possibilities we outlined above.[19] With this expansion of the double guarding in mind, we can well understand the prime motivation for Rabbi Kluger's resistance to modern technology's twin challenges contained within its mass means of production—the effective removal of quality control from the individual product and the separation of the craftsman from his handiwork.[20] The former represents a clear danger to the requirement to guard each *Matzah* from *Hametz*; the latter is a serious and perhaps fatal impediment to the guarding of intent. The machine process of baking is more than a difficulty for a formalized set of rules; it represents a movement away from that inner dynamic of *Halakha* which is the oft quoted statement of *Rav Hai Gaon* (939–1038) which admits that while "an Israelite is permitted to eat matzah baked by a Gentile under the proper supervision of an Israelite, nevertheless men of [exemplary] deeds, the pious and those who are stringent upon themselves, will themselves knead and bake [the *matzah*]. . . ."[21]

The first part of the responsum assessing the delitorious effect that replacing the hand baking with machines would have upon the poor is what Rabbi Kluger considers his "first and foremost" reason for prohibiting that innovation. Furthermore, the last three reasons (previously discussed) are introduced by the phrase 'aside from this [concern for this poor which mandates retention of handbaking]' clearly labelling them as secondary to the ethical considerations not only in chronology but in their contribution to decision making. Dr. Ellenson, nevertheless, considers that the "moral considerations advanced by Kluger are *ultimately divre musar*, words of ethical sensitivity, which, while important, possess, in the end, a secondary status." He sees this as evidenced by its being bolstered by a legal text from the Babylonian Talmud (i.e., Megillah 46) that functions as a "statutory case. Within Halakha, Ellenson observes, ethical values never exist as "independent standards" with a "claim to authority."

Upon examination this case cited as an analogy by Rabbi Kluger proves the opposite. The obligation to read the Megillah on the day Purim falls including the Sabbath "is an obligation which stems from the Oral Tradition *(divre Kabbalah)*."[22] *Its postponement from the Sabbath is not put forth on the basis of any legal text or any argumentation but according to Rabbi Kluger they solely "cancelled it on account of the poor who anxiously await the reading of the Megillah* (and who cannot for logistical reasons attend its reading on the Sabbath)."

Rabbi Kluger employs that tenet in our own case to maintain the radical thrust of this ethical imperative concern for the poor would by analogy, Rabbi Kluger implies, override the use of machines even if the latter had a compelling obligatory basis (as reading the Megillah in its proper time does). But the fact is that there is not the "least adhesion to a mitzvah" (my translation) in machine baking, lacking any religious claim which the ethical consideration for the poor needs even to contend with. This is a relevant point for if one attempts to demonstrate—as Rabbi Nathanson did, reading the situation differently than Rabbi Kluger but generally agreeing with the same legal principles—the machine process does not impair the guarding for intent and that it significantly improves the guarding from *hametz*, this would render its use preferable for ritual reasons.[23] Rabbi Kluger makes it clear, that nonetheless, ethical concern for the poor would even override any such ritual argument.

Having established this power of the ethical concern for the poor within Jewish decision making, Rabbi Kluger now moves to solidify it through institutionalization. Here, ritual, law and ethics converge. Rabbi Kluger ingeniously identifies handbaking with the practice of *Meot itim* (literally, "money for wheat," that is the special charity collection for Passover necessities) which is customary among (the people) Israel and the source of which is derived from the words of the early medieval rabbinic authorities *(rishonim)*." Motivated by sensitivity to the plight of the needy, the Jerusalem Talmud[24] regulated how the communities, *if they elected to do so*, should levy a special tax from its citizens and to whom it should be distributed. By the time of the *Or Zarua* (1180–1250)[25] this tax developed into an established "custom for communities" to exercise. As an authorized yearly tax this custom had the formality of law with ethical considerations emerging to soften some of its formal requirements.[26] Eventually this customary community tax evolved into a *personal obligation*[27] mandating all individuals to contribute their fair share seemingly irrespective of what the community does or mandates.

This triumph for personalizing and deepening ethical obligation evidently did not fare well in Brody where "a number of middle-class householders and, all the more so, common people, do not contribute *Me'ot Hitim*" (my emendation of Ellenson's translation). While Rabbi Kluger would have obviously preferred that people discharge their ethical obligations fully and directly, he was able to consider the handbaking process which benefitted the poor as a contemporary—if second rate—manifestation of *Me'ot Hitim*.

The baking of *matzah* is in itself not a commandment—it has no blessing before it and no sanctity accrues to the resulting product. It is merely the way in which one prepares an item to be used for ritual purpose. But given the precise requirements for baking, the guarding from the ever present danger of *Hametz* and the need for a continual manifestation of intent, it is akin to a ritual act. Indeed the baking process did gain that aura within pietistic circles.[28] Infused with this new designation of *Me'otHitim*, handbaking is *Halakhically* fully institutionalized as a ritual. Rabbi Kluger, at the end of the responsum, can now refer to it as 'a custom of your fathers.' And as an established custom it has been rendered impregnable from attack by any competitor.

Does Rabbi Kluger function in this case as a ritual judge, moral authority or religious leader? The answer would seem to be all three. This is due to the nature of the decision-making that needed to be brought into play here. Rabbi Kluger was responding not merely to a problem of limited *Halakhic* analysis concerning the presence or absence of leaven in machine made *matzah* but more fully to *a question of public policy—whether to employ a new procedure which would have immense legal-ritual, religious and ethical repercussions*. He functioned as a judge but also as a Rabbi whose role in the words of the pre-eminent scholar-rabbi of the subsequent generation is "to redress the grievances of those who are abandoned and alone, to protect the dignity of the poor, and to save the oppressed from the hands of the oppressor."[29] As a question of public policy, the decision making process utilizes halakhic reasoning in dialectical relation to ethical sensitivity, along with ritual considerations and religious feeling.

If Rabbi Kluger found little difficulty in synthesizing these apparently disparate elements it is due in some measure to the inner connections of ethics, religiosity and law found within Passover and *matzah* ritual and symbolism. The Bible characterizes *matzah* as *lehem 'Oni*—'bread of affliction' (Deut. XVI:3). The Talmud renders it (among other readings) as *lehem 'ani*—poor bread. This is taken in two ways: either as bread that is poor containing only flour and water as opposed to the enriched *Matzah ashirah;* or the bread of those who are poor.[30] In both sense poverty and *matzah* are intertwined.

The seder ritual exemplifies historic identification with the poor and powerless. "We were slaves of Pharoah in Egypt" is a recurrent theme of its liturgy. There is also a motif of emulation of the poor in the preparation of *matzah* as found in the conclusion of Rav Hai Gaon's observations on the minimal and the ideal standards:

> An Israelite is permitted to eat *matzah* baked by a Gentile under the proper supervision of an Israelite, nevertheles men of [exemplary] deeds, the pious and those who are stringent upon themselves, will themselves knead and bake the matzah and this is what is meant: *"Poor Bread"—just as it [The Talmud] says: "just as a poor man fires [the oven] and his wife bakes, so here too, he [the observant] heats, and she bakes."*

The Halakha moves beyond identification and emulation of the poor—which left alone could mean excessive idealization and quieticism—to active concern for their plight. This concern lies within the celebration of all the holidays. As Maimonides puts it:

When one eats and drinks [on the Holidays, in fulfillment of the commandment of celebrating its joy] he is obligated to feed the stranger, the orphan and widow along with the rest of the wretched poor. But one who locks the doors of his courtyard and eats and drinks, along with his children and wife, and does not feed and give drink to the poor and'those of embittered spirits—theirs is not a [celebration of the] joy of the commandment but rather a [celebration of the joy] of one's belly.[31]

The ethos of Passover, the feast of liberation, is this preoccupation with the poor. The declaration "all who are hungry let them enter and eat" begins the seder rite and in a real way permeates the entire holiday. Additionally, the memory of the Egyptian experience is the source of the obligation to protect the powerless in society—the stranger, the widow, the orphan and the poor.[32] Rabbi Kluger's refusal to rely upon the Westernized German community for sanction to *initiate* a new technological procedure was not a kneejerk reaction against modernity.[33] It was ultimately a decision that the preparation of poor bread should benefit the poor and not be enriched by their very lifeblood.

NOTES

[1] *Mekilta de Rabbi Ishmael*. translated and edited by Jacob Z. Lauterbach. Philadelphia: Jewish Publication Society of America. 1933. p.144.

[2] *Ibid*, 148.

[3] Out of fear of it becoming *hametz* on Passover.

[4] Talmud Bavli Pesahim 38b.

[5] *Ibid.*, Rashi.

[6] Pesahim 40a. See the attendant *Rishonim*.

[7] *Ritbah*. The best discussion of this topic is found in *Sdei Hemed* of Hayim Medmi: Hametz U'matzah 13; *Ha Moadim ba Halakhah* by Rabbi S. Y. Zevin (Jerusalem, 1957); *Mikrai Kodesh Pesah* by Rabbi Z.P. Frank (Jerusalem, 1976/76); *Haggadah Mo'adim U-Zemanim*, by Rabbi M. Sternbukh (Jerusalem, 1979/80).

[8] *Rashi; Rosh, Pesahim* Chapter II, 26; *Teshuvot Ha Rosh* 14:4.

[9] *Rif*, see discussion in *Ritvah*, and *Ran*.

[10] *Ramban, Pesahim* 40a; also *Sefer Ha-Manhig, Dinei Matzah*.

[11] *Otzar ha-Geonim* edited by Dr. B. M. Lewin (Jerusalem, 1930) Vol. III, Peashim 40a, 112–115.

[12] *The Symbolism of Evil* (Beacon, 1967), p. 136.

[13] *Pesahim* 40a.

[14] *Hagahot Maimaniyot Hilhot Hamets U'matzah*, Chapter V, note 8.

[15] Rif following Raba. Note *Maharam Halavah* on *Pesahim* 40a.

[16] *Otzar ha-Gaonim*, 118–120; also *Sefer Raviyah Pesahim* 40a.

[17] His position follows that of the *Shulchan Aruch*.

[18] In this sense, there is no distinction between ritual and ethical practice. Both assume the law to be a minimum to be transcended.

[19] The custom of only eating *matzah* guarded with intent the entire holiday; of not eating gebrukt (*matzah* which after baking came into contact with liquids [see *Keneset Ha-Gadolah*].

[20] *War and Human Progress, an Essay on the Rise of Industrial Civilization* by J. U. Nef (Cambridge, Mass., 1950); *A History of the Economic Institutions of Modern Europe* by F. A. Nussbaum (New York, 1933).

[21] *Otzar ha-Gaonim*, 121. See also quotation in *Rosh*.

[22] I read this differently than Ellenson. The confusion arises from *hiyub, me-divrei* and *u'Batluhu* all being preceded by a *vav* (and). It would seem that the first two phrases together refer to the practice of reading the scroll on the 15th of *Adar*. The term *hiyub* refers to the nature of the *mitzvah* to be performed—that it is an *obligation* and not a matter of choice. The phrase *me-divrei kabbalah*, then tells of the source of that obligation—that it is *from the Oral Tradition*, and not only a custom. The third term *u'Batluhu* is then the whole point—that despite its firm grounding in law, they *cancelled it* anyway.

[23] This was the argument of Zvi Pesah Frank, Chief Rabbi of Jerusalem in the early 20th century.

[24] *Talmud Yerushalmi Baba Batra* 1:4.

[25] *Or Zaru'a, Pesahim*, 255.

[26] *Mogen Avraham* on Shulhan 'Arukh 429; sources cited there.

[27] *Pri Megadim* on above.

[28] Some repopulized the almost dormant custom of baking the matzah on the day (the 14th of Nissan) directly preceding Passover, seeing it as a substitute for the slaughtering of the Paschal Lamb. The Tchnernobler *Hassidim*, on this basis recited the festive *Hallel* with a blessing as they did so as was the practice with the Paschal Lamb. This was an extreme disruption of normative Halakhic practice. See *Halakhot V'Halikhot Ba Hassidut* by A. Wertheim. (Mossad Ha Rav Kook, Jerusalem, 1960), pp. 172–73.

[29] *Halakhic Man* by Joseph B. Soloveitchik (Jewish Publication Society of America, 1983), p. 91.

[30] *Pesahim* 36a, 116a.

[31] *Hilkhot Yom Tov* 6:18.

[32] One example from many is Deut. XXV:14–22. See also "The Laws Regarding Slavery" by E. E. Urbach in *Papers of the Institute of Jewish Studies, London*, ed. J. G. Weiss (Jerusalem, 1964).

[33] In this last section on ritual we are engaged in what Clifford Geertz would describe as a hermeneutic enterprise "one in which ideas are used as a more or less handy way into understanding the social institutions and cultural formulations that surround them and give them meaning." "Local Knowledge: Fact and Law in Comparative Perspective" in *Local Knowledge* (Basic Books, 1983), pp. 186–87).

WORKS CONSULTED

Ackroyd, Peter R. "Continuity and Discontinuity: Rehabilitation and Authentication." pp. 215–34 in *Tradition and Theology in the Old Testament,* ed. Douglas A. Knight. Philadelphia: Fortress Press; London: SPCK, 1977.

Agassi, Joseph. "Conventions of Knowledge in Talmudic Law." *Journal of Jewish Studies* 25 (February): 6–34.

Ahlström, G. W. *Royal Administration and National Religion in Ancient Palestine.* Leiden: E. J. Brill, 1982.

Aiken, Henry David. *Reason and Conduct: New Bearings in Moral Philosophy.* New York: Alfred A. Knopf, 1962.

Barr, James. *Old and New in Interpretation: A Study of the Two Testaments.* London: SCM, 1966.

Berger, Peter L., and Thomas Luckmann. *The Social Construction of Reality: A Treatise in the Sociology of Knowledge.* Garden City: Doubleday, 1967.

Berger, Peter. "A Sociological View of the Secularization of Theology." *Journal for the Scientific Study of Religion* 6:1 (1967).

Borowitz, Eugene. "The Authority of the Ethical Impulse in Halakha." In Jonathan V. Plaut, ed., *Through the Sound of Many Voices: Writings Contributed on the Occasion of the Seventieth Birthday of W. Gunther Plaut.* Toronto, 1982.

Cardozo, Benjamin. *The Nature of the Judicial Process.* New Haven: Yale University Press, 1977.

Carlson, R. A. *David, the Chosen King: A Traditio-Historical Approach to the Second Book of Samuel.* Stockholm: Almqvist & Wiksell, 1964.

Coats, George W. "Parable, Fable, and Anecdote: Storytelling in the Succession Narrative." *Interpretation* 35 (1981) 368–82.

Crüsemann, Frank. *Der Widerstand gegen das Königtum: Die antiköniglichen Texte des Alten Testaments und der Kampf um den frühen israelitischen Staat.* Wissenschaftliche Monographien zum Alten und Neuen Testament, 49. Neukirchen-Vluyn: Neukirchener Verlag, 1978.

Dorff, Elliot. "The Interaction of Jewish Law and Morality." *Judaism* 26:4(Fall, 1977): 455–466.

Dorff, Elliot. "Judaism as a Religious Legal System." *Hastings Law Journal* 29:6 (July 1978).

Dworkin, Ronald M. (ed.) "Is Law a System of Rules." *The Philosophy of Law*, ed. Ronald Dworkin. Oxford: Oxford University Press, 1977.

Farley, Edward. *Ecclesial Reflection: An Anatomy of Theological Method*. Philadelphia: Fortress Press, 1982.

Feldman, David. *Marital Relations, Birth Control and Abortion in Jewish Law*. New York: Schocken, 1974.

Fishbane, Michael. "Torah and Tradition." pp. 275–300 in *Tradition and Theology in the Old Testament*, ed. Douglas A. Knight. Philadelphia: Fortress Press; London: SPCK, 1977.

Fishbane, Michael. *Text and Texture: Close Readings of Selected Biblical Texts*. New York: Schocken Books, 1979.

Flanagan, James W. "Court History or Succession Document? A Study of 2 Samuel 9–20 and 1 Kings 1–2." *Journal of Biblical Literature* 91 (1972) 172–81.

Frankel, Jonah. "Hermeneutic Problems in the Study of the Aggadic Literature." *Tarbiz* 47:139–72.

Freehof, Solomon. *The Responsa Literature*. Philadelphia: Jewish Publication Society, 1955.

Frost, Mervyn. "Justice and the Nature of Legal Argumentation." *Logique et Analyse* ns 14 (53–54): 279–288.

Geertz, Clifford. *The Interpretation of Cultures*. New York: Basic Books, 1973.

Green, William S. ""What's in a Name" The Problematic of Rabbinic 'Biography'" in W. S. Green, ed. *Approaches to the Study of Ancient Judaism*. Chico, CA: Scholars Press, pp. 77–92.

Green, William S. "Palestinian Holy Men: Charismatic Leadership and Rabbinic Tradition." *Aufstieg und Nierdergang der Romischen Welt*, edited by Hildegard Temporini and Wolfgang Haase, Vol. 19:2, pp. 619–47. Berlin: Walter DeGruyter.

Green, William S. *The Traditions of Joshua ben Hananiah. Part I: The Early Traditions*. Leiden: E. J. Brill, 1981.

Green, William S. "Reading and Writing of Rabbinism: Toward an Interpretation of Rabbinic Literature." *JAAR* 51 (June, 1983): 191–106.

Gunn, D. M. *The Story of King David: Genre and Interpretation*. Journal for the Study of the Old Testament Supplement Series, 6. Sheffield: JSOT, The University of Sheffield, 1978.

Gustafson, James M. *Christian Ethics and the Community*. Philadelphia: Pilgrim Press, 1971.

Halpern, Baruch. *The Constitution of the Monarchy in Israel*. Harvard Semitic Monographs, 25. Chico: Scholars Press, 1981.

Harrod, Howard L. *The Human Center: Moral Agency in the Social World*. Philadelphia: Fortress Press, 1981.

Hauerwas, Stanley. "The Moral Authority of Scripture: The Politics and Ethics of Remembering." *Interpretation* 34 (1980): 356–70.

Ishida, Tomoo. *The Royal Dynasties in Ancient Israel: A Study on the Formation and Development of Royal-Dynastic Ideology.* Beiheft zur Zeitschrift für die alttestamentliche Wissenschaft, 142. Berlin and New York: Walter de Gruyter, 1977.

Ishida, Tomoo. "Solomon's Succession to the Throne of David—A Political Analysis." pp. 175–87 in *Studies in the Period of David and Solomon and Other Essays*, ed. Tomoo Ishida. Winona Lake: Eisenbrauns, 1982.

Jackson, Bernard. "Legalism." *Journal of Jewish Studies* 30 (Spring):1–22.

Jacob, Edmond. "Histoire et historiens dans l'Ancien Testament." *Revue d'histoire et de philosophie religieuses* 35 (1955): 26–34.

Jacobs, Louis. *Theology in the Responsa.* London and Boston, 1975.

Kadushin, Max. *The Rabbinic Mind.* New York, 1952.

Kanter, Shammai. *Rabban Gamaliel II: The Legal Traditions.* Chico: Scholars Press, 1980.

Kearns, Thomas R. "Open Texture and Judicial Law-making." *Social Theory and Practice* 2 (Fall): 177–188.

Kellner, Menachem. *Contemporary Jewish Ethics.* New York: Sanhedrin, 1978.

Knight, Douglas A. *Rediscovering the Traditions of Israel.* Rev. ed. Society of Biblical Literature Dissertation Series, 9. Missoula: Scholars Press, 1975.

Knight, Douglas A. "Jeremiah and the Dimensions of the Moral Life." pp. 87–105 in *The Divine Helmsman: Studies on God's Control of Human Events, Presented to Lou H. Silberman,* ed. James L. Crenshaw and Samuel Sandmel. New York: Ktav, 1980.

Ladd, John. *The Structure of a Moral Code.* Cambridge, Mass.: Harvard University Press, 1957.

McCarter, P. Kyle, Jr. "'Plots, True or False': The Succession Narrative as Court Apologetic." *Interpretation* 35 (1981) 355–67.

Mettinger, Tryggve N. D. *Solomonic State Officials: A Study of the Civil Government Officials of the Israelite Monarchy.* Coniectanea biblica, Old Testament Series, 5. Lund: CWK Gleerup, 1971.

Mettinger, Tryggve N. D. *King and Messiah: The Civil and Sacral Legitimation of the Israelite Kings.* Coniectanea biblica, Old Testament Series, 8. Lund: CWK Gleerup, 1976.

Miller, Bruce L. "Open Texture and Judicial Decisions." *Social Theory and Practice* 2 (Fall): 163–176.

Mowinckel, Sigmund. "Israelite Historiography." *Annual of the Swedish Theological Institute* 2 (1963) 4–26.

Neusner, Jacob. *The Rabbinic Traditions about the Pharisees before 70.* Vols. 1–3. Leiden: E. J. Brill, 1971.

Neusner, Jacob. *Eliezer ben Hyrcanus: The Tradition and the Man.* Vols. 1–2. Leiden: E. J. Brill, 1973.

Neusner, Jacob. "Ritual without Myth: The Use of Legal Materials for the Study of Religions." *Religion* 5 (Autumn, 1975):91–100.

Neusner, Jacob. *A History of the Mishnaic Law of Purities. The Redaction and Formulation of the Order of Purities in Mishnah and Tosefta.* Leiden: E. J. Brill, 1974–77.

Neusner, Jacob. *Judaism: The Evidence of the Mishnah.* Chicago: University of Chicago Press, 1981.

Newman, Louis E. *The Sanctity of the Seventh Year: A Study of Mishnah Tractate Shebiit.* Chico: Scholars Press, 1983.

Noth, Martin. *Überlieferungsgeschichtliche Studien: Die sammelnden und bearbeitenden Geschichtswerke im Alten Testament.* Halle: Niemeyer, 1943. 3d. ed., 1967 = *The Deuteronomistic History.* [Translation of first half of German original.] Journal for the Study of the Old Testament Supplement Series, 15. Sheffield: University of Sheffield Department of Biblical Studies, 1981.

Noth, Martin. *Könige*, vol. 1. Biblischer Kommentar, Altes Testament, IX/1. Neukirchen-Vluyn: Neukirchener Verlag, 1968.

Perelman, Chaim. *The Idea of Justice and the Problem of Argument.* trans. by John Petrie. New York: The Humanities Press, 1963.

Pospisil, Leonard. *Anthropology of Law: A Comparative Theory.* New York: Harper and Row, 1971.

Powell, James M., ed. *Medieval Studies.* Syracuse, New York, 1976.

von Rad, Gerhard. "Die Anfang der Geschichtsschreibung im alten Israel." *Archiv für Kulturgeschichte* 32 (1944) 1–42. = pp. 148–88 in *Gesammelte Studien zum Alten Testament.* Theologische Buchereri, 8. Munich: Chr. Kaiser Verlag, 1965. = "The Beginnings of Historical Writing in Ancient Israel." pp. 166–204 in *The Problem of the Hexateuch, and Other Essays.* Edinburgh/London: Oliver & Boyd, 1966.

Richards, David A. J. *The Moral Criticism of the Law.* Encino and Belmont, CA., 1977.

Ricoeur, Paul. *The Symbolism of Evil.* Beacon, 1967.

Rosner, Fred and Bleich, J. David. *Jewish Bioethics.* New York: Sanhedrin Press, 1979.

Rost, Leonard. *Die Überlieferung von der Thronnachfolge Davids.* Beiträge zur Wissenschaft vom Alten und Neuen Testament, III/6. Stuttgart: W. Kohlhammer, 1926. = pp. 119–253 in *Das kleine Credo und andere Studien zum Alten Testament.* Heidelberg: Quelle & Meyer, 1965.

Roth, Sol. "Methodology and Social Policy: A Jewish Perspective." In *The Formation of Social Policy in the Catholic and Jewish Traditions*, edited by Eugene J. Fisher and Daniel F. Polish, pp. 147–61. Notre Dame: University of Notre Dame Press, 1980.

Schutz, Alfred. *Reflections on the Problem of Relevance.* Ed. Richard Zaner. New Haven/London: Yale University Press, 1970.

Smend, Rudolf. "Tradition and History: A Complex Relation." pp. 49–68 in *Tradition and Theology in the Old Testament*, ed. Douglas A. Knight. Philadelphia: Fortree Press; London: SPCK, 1977.

Smith, Morton. "The So-Called 'Biography of David' in the Books of Samuel and Kings." *Harvard Theological Review* 44 (1951) 167–69.

Soloveitchik, Joseph B. *Halakhic Man*. Philadelphia: Jewish Publication Society, 1983.

Spero, Shubert. *Morality, Halakha, and Jewish Tradition*. New York, 1983.

Tadmor, Hayim. "Traditional Institutions and the Monarchy: Social and Political Tensions in the Time of David and Solomon." pp. 239–57 in *Studies in the Period of David and Solomon and Other Essays*, ed. Tomoo Ishida. Winona Lake: Eisenbrauns, 1982.

Twersky, Isadore. *Introduction to the Code of Maimonides*. New Haven and London: 1980.

Unger, Rudolf. *Literaturgeschichte als Problemgeschichte: Zur Frage geisteshistorischer Synthese, mit besonderer Beziehung auf Wilhelm Dilthey*. Berlin: Deutsche Verlagsgesellschaft für Politik und Geschichte, 1924.

Veijola, Timo. *Die ewige Dynastie: David und die Entstehung seiner Dynastie nach der deuteronomistischen Darstellung*. Helsinki: Suomalainen Tiedeakatemia, 1975.

Waldenberg, Eliezer Judah. *Ziz Eliezer*. Volume X. Jerusalem, 1970.

Wellek, René, and Austin Warren. *Theory of Literature*. 3d ed. New York/London: Harcourt Brace Jovanovich, 1975.

Wharton, James A. "A Plausible Tale: Story and Theology in II Samuel 9–20, I Kings 1–2." *Interpretation* 35 (1981) 341–54.

Whybray, R. N. *The Succession Narrative: A Study of II Samuel 9–20 and I Kings 1 and 2*. Studies in Biblical Theology, II/9. London: SCM, 1968.

Wrobleski, Jerzy. "Justification of Legal Decisions." *Revue Internationale de Philosophie* 33 (127–128): 277–293.

Würthwein, Ernst. *Die Erzählung von der Thronfolge Davids—Theologische oder politische Geschichtsschreibung?* Zurich: Theologischer Verlag, 1974.

www.ingramcontent.com/pod-product-compliance
Lightning Source LLC
Chambersburg PA
CBHW032301150426
43195CB00008BA/528